2018 U

Certified Coins Sold at Auction

By Stan McDonald
Comprehensive and unsurpassed

Last Updated 8.27.2017

Introduction
After 18 years, this coin guide remains the most comprehensive and unsurpassed in its ability to provide an extensive number of encapsulated coin errors as recognized by the world leading coin experts from ANA, PCGS, and NGC. No other coin guide presents final auction prices which will give collectors true values.

This guide contains over 1,000 plus certified coin errors. Off-Center coins and other error types are included in Chapter 14.

Contacts:
Stan.McDonald@coinerrorguide on twitter
McDonald.Stan@comcast.net

Searching for coins in circulation that contain errors can be a rewarding experience. Pocket change, bank rolled coin, and looking through old collections are some of the sources for error coin seekers.
To aid the collector, photographs of modern day error coins are provided in this book as a reference. The large number of error coins makes it impossible to photograph all types listed in this book.
While most coin series contain error coins, almost every Lincoln cent year contains an error type. No other series contains as many errors impacted by using and reworking dies until they were no longer useable. By reworking dies, the mint would have some doubling resulting in re-punching the mint mark and creating a D over D, or an S over S. Some of the dies that were not used at one mint location were often shipped to another location where the mint mark was removed from the die and another placed on the die. By

attempting to remove a mint mark, sometimes the process was incomplete and thus coins were minted showing two mint marks a S over D, or a D over S. These errors to the collecting community are referred to as OMM (Over mint-mark) and RPM (Repunched mint mark).

Most doubled die coins have very clear doubling with the bulk of the doubling in the date, the mintmark, or the word "LIBERTY." Included in this book is an artist's depiction of true doubling verses machine doubling. The collector can use the drawing as a concise method of ensuring that the doubling is authentic.

Above is a sample of the doubling of a Lincoln cent. This doubled die was created by the misaligning the reworking of the die into the master die. Detailed photographs are shown in a later chapter for coins that can be located in circulation today.

This edition includes some errors struck on incorrect planchets. Error coins minted on planchets not intended for the minting of the coin are called mules[1]. As evidenced by the numerous planchet errors bought and sold recently, the US Mint still creates many error coins with one denomination stamped on another.

There is a distinct difference between a machine double coin and true doubled die coin and the collector needs to be aware of the difference. Our reference guide can validate the error and show the range of values as realized at auctions. Some error coins have a wide range of final sale prices in the same grade and with the same encapsulation service. At auction, collectors bid for coins based on the desire to acquire a particular error coin. Some coin errors, like the 1972 doubled die Lincoln cent have a wide range of auction price results. There is often overlapping with pricing from one grade to the next. This reference guide will give the

---

[1] Mules – Coins minted on planchets not intended for the particular mintage.

2

collector the opportunity to understand the price ranges of coins and the overlap of prices from one grade to the next. Below are the auction results for the Lincoln cent 1972,72 over 72. Note the overlap between MS64 and MS65 and the wide range of auction prices.

Lincoln Cent
1972 72 over 72
(ANACS MS63, $175) (ANACS MS64, $59-$460) (ANACS MS65, $190-$662) (PCGS MS66, $718-$1,122) (NGC MS67, $2,245)

Table of Contents

Preface

This book provides the coin collector with a detailed description of the following:

- The minting process from US Mint sources
- A detailed description of mint error classifications with photographs.
- A comprehensive listing with over 850 US error coins as cataloged by PCGS, ANACS, and NGC and sold at major auctions.
- A comprehensive value guide by date and error type.
- Many photographs of modern day coin errors.

There are thousands error coins that have been encapsulated by PCGS, NGC, and ANACS. Many coin errors are very valuable while others sell for less than the cost the coin encapsulation.

Error coins can have a wide range of sales prices for the same dated coin with the same grade and error type. It is difficult to understand why a coin with the same date, error, and grade encapsulated by the same coin service can have a wide range of selling prices. This book presents a range of prices paid at auctions for each auctioned coin.

The findings of certified error coins sold at auction is the content of this book. In 2014, we started listing newly added coin errors with the year "20xx noted next to the find so that the collector can identify what has been discovered most recently. As we find already listed error coins with additional grades and prices, we add them to this book without notation.

We do not list raw coins not certified by PCGS[2], NCG[3], or ANACS[4] so that what we list is only authenticated error coins. We recognize that there are other coin encapsulation services; however, they are not as revered by collectors and we will not add any of these findings to this book.

It is very possible that one grading service can grade a coin lower or higher than another service. Experts in grading may at times take one coin graded by a service, and have it re-graded by another service with success of obtaining a higher

---

[2] PCGS – A certification service of encapsulated coins. Professional Coin Grading Service.

[3] NGC – A certification service – Numismatic Guarantee Corporation.

[4] ANACS – An encapsulation coin service established in 1972. -American Numismatic Association

grade. In some cases, this could be a difference of several thousand dollars.

As an avid collector for 50 years, I have bought and sold thousands of US coins at auction. My interest in coins has led to the publication of coin guides based upon completed auction results from major auction companies, live auctions, and coin shows. No other coin guide provides this information. This book has been selling on Amazon and Barnes and Noble since 2000 with much success.

Over the years, I have seen thousands of coins that are missed struck, and off center. Some coins sold for thousands while others sold for less than $100.

For the fortunate few that stumble across a true rare error, the reward can be very profitable. Error coin collecting has increased in popularity since the 1970's when collectors began to establish collections of errors. Thousands of coins are in circulation and in private collections that go undiscovered with the types of errors described in this book.

The evidence for coins that have circulated before the coin error discovery is with the coins that are graded in extra fine and lower conditions by the major encapsulation services. There are thousands of examples of error coins graded in good through extra fine condition and many of these coins are worth hundreds of dollars, if not thousands of dollars.

It takes a lot of patience to search through thousands of coins in order to pick out a coin that meets the standard to be classified as an error coin. Over the years, I searched though thousands coins seeking to find some of the elusive error coins such as the 1969-S doubled die Lincoln cent that can sell upwards of $20,000. I am still looking.

Chapter 1 – Classifications of Coin Varieties

There are three categories of error coins as provided by ANA[5]. Metal usage and striking errors refer widely as "planchet[6] errors", and die errors. The third type is mint striking errors. This does not include the varieties[7] that the US Mint has issued over the years.

The modern day method of minting coins is to punch the coin stock in the size and configuration for stamping first. For cents, sheet stock in circular arrangement is used and then the surface and edge are prepared for minting. The blanks enter the dies for stamping and the obverse and reverse of the coin.

Since the inception of coin collecting, there has been much controversy over what constitutes a true mint error.

We cannot emphasize enough the importance of obtaining a professional opinion concerning the type of error and the potential value of the error before sending it to an encapsulation service. If you believe, you have an error coin the best practice is to bring it to a coin dealer that is certified as an ANA and or PNG[8] dealer to obtain an opinion.

Planchet Errors

The word "planchet" is a term used by the US Mint and coin collectors for the blank and the blanks with upsets on the edge of the coin. A type I planchet is the blank itself. A type II planchet is the blank with the edging rolled on it. The type of planchet error is important in the classification of error coins and the value of the coins.

An improper alloy mixture constitutes a coin error. For example, a sheet of stock used for the minting of cents may have the incorrect proportion of copper and zinc in places that create some coins with uneven layers of the different metals. There are cases of Roosevelt dimes that are missing the nickel layer on the surface of the coin, thus a Roosevelt

---

[5] ANA – American Numismatic Association
[6] Planchet – The raw blank that the mint uses to press the coin details.
[7] Variety - A coin of the same date and basic design as another but with slight differences. PCGS recognizes all major varieties while there are thousands of minor varieties, most of which have significance only to specialists of the particular series. After hubbed dies, introduced in the 1840s, varieties are mainly variations in date and mintmark size and placement. (from the PCGS glossary)
[8] PNG – Professional Numismatics Guild

dime minted on a copper alloy planchet. In addition, there have been cases of Lincoln cents missing the copper surface revealing a coin minted on a zinc planchet.
Using the incorrect planchet in the minting process is another form of error. For example, a Quarter minted using a dime coin blank.

Above is a Washington quarter struck on a dime planchet

Mule Error
This is a rare Mint error where the obverse die is of one coin and the reverse die is of another coin. The most famous of the Mule errors is a Sacagawea dollar/Washington quarter Mule, where a Washington quarter obverse is paired with a Sacagawea reverse.[9]

---

[9] PCGS definition

Washington quarter obverse with a Sacagawea reverse.

Transitional Error
A coin minted on a planchet from a metal change such as a copper to zinc transitional error. One of the most valuable Lincoln cents is the 1943 minted on a copper planchet. This is a true transitional error.

Clipped Planchets
A planchet error also refers to many types of issues with obtaining a perfect blank for minting. Many of these planchet errors are missing portions of the edge of the coin or most of the planchet itself. The most common error is a planchet that results in a half moon. Coins missing part of the planchet are "clipped" planchets. Some of the planchet errors can be severe with various types of missing pieces of the coin and classified as curved clips, bowtie clips, assay clips etc. The most common clip is the curved clip as shown below:

1982-P Roosevelt Dime clipped planchet

Lamination Error

A dirty or oily blank may cause the details of the coin to become dull or even missing. A piece of debris may find its way into the dies causing a series of lines minted on the surface of the coin.

A lamination error results when the coin surface is peeling or cracking. Lamination errors are normally not of significant value; however, there are collectors that value these coins and they will pay a premium for unusual types of lamination issues.

Above is a 1943 Jefferson nickel with a lamination error

Planchet Stock Errors

Planchet errors created from uneven stock makes the coin thicker or thinner than intended. The weight of the coin verses the normal intended weight contributes to the value of the coin. Thousands of Lincoln cents range in thickness from one end of the coin to the other. These are not of any significant value.

Die Errors
Die errors are those caused by the mint dies wearing down over time, broken dies, or dies that have not been prepared identical to the original replaced dies. The result of some dies errors are cuds, and die cracks.

Dies that wear down over time may result in coin missing the finer details. These are not die errors. Jefferson nickels minted before the 1990's, for example, have a tendency to be missing the lines in the steps on the reverse of the coin. Some early dated Jefferson nickels with full steps are valued in the thousands because of the rarity related to the poor minting process.

Many collectors are only interested in the grade of a coin and not the specific details of full steps for a Jefferson nickel or full torch lines for a Roosevelt dime. The full torch designation began in the late 1990's by PCGS. Thousands of Roosevelt dimes exist in older holders that do not include the full torch designation. We have found that the full torch designation for Roosevelt dimes has not attracted much attention from the collecting community that would result in premiums paid for full torch Roosevelt dimes. The full line detail in the Franklin half liberty bell does have a major impact in the value of the coin, especially in the highest MS grades.

Die Crack
When the mint die suffers a fracture and this crack feature transposes onto the coins in the minting process. Coins minted with a die crack have a thin line or lines raised running across the surface of the coin. Below is a photograph show how a die crack results in a raised line on the surface of the coin. Note the horizontal lines running through the vines.

Die Cud

A die cud occurs when part of the die breaks away and the metal flows into the break in the minting process. Below is a cud error on a Lincoln cent. Most die cuds are not extremely valuable because of the commonality.

Brockage

Brockage refers to a type of error coin in which one side of the coin has the normal design and the other side has a mirror image of the same design impressed upon it.

Above is a 1952 Washington quarter with brockage

RPM's/RPD's/OMM's/MPD's

Before 1990, all US coin dies were subject to mintmark errors resulting from the preparation of the dies. Hammering the mint-mark into the die manually sometimes causing a die to have a doubling. In the minting process, this would create a series of coins with a distinct of slight doubling of the mintmark. Hundreds of these errors can be located on the internet for sale noted as RPM's[10]. There are also RPD's[11] (re-punched dated coins); some of which are very valuable. RPD's have the date punched over the tops of the numbers of the raised date. These errors are not actual doubling of the date but raised lines are on the numbers indicating multiple dates struck over the original date.

A number of notable error coins exist with one mintmark on the die punched over another mintmark. The mint intentionally used one die, in this case a San Francisco mint die and converted this die to a Denver mint die. These coins are over mintmark errors, or OMM.[12] One OMM Lincoln cent of note is the 1944-D over S mintage.

Some coins discovered with dates that appear multiple times in various locations on the coin are MPD's[13] (misplaced dates). MPD's are extremely rare.

A repunched mintmark is the result of a skilled mint worker hammering in a mintmark on the coin manually to repair it. Coin dies used before 1986 required rework to continue using them. When the mint worker hammered in the mintmark to rework it, sometimes the alignment was off creating a doubling or an RPM.

True doubled die coins result with a missed alignment of the die to hub. The hub is the master die.

---

[10] RPM – Re-punched mint mark
[11] RPD – re-punched date
[12] OMM – Over mint mark
[13] MPD – Misplaced date

14

Above is a typical RPM – 1938-D over D Buffalo Nickel

Doubled dies

Coins designated as doubled dies are the result of imperfect dies prepared from the master hub. Dies are impressed on the master hub several times in order to create a working die for minting coins. Doubling occurs when there is a misalignment of the impressions.

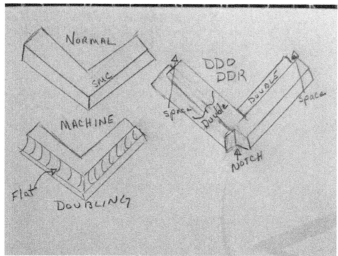

Above is the author's rendition of hub doubling and machine doubling on coins.

The normal lettering and dates shown above in the upper left. The machine doubling shown below and to the left reveals flat doubling. The drawing in the upper right shows notches and spaces with the doubling the same height as the normal letter and numbering.

The classification of a doubled die coin can be a very difficult task for those professionals that try to determine if a coin is a true doubled die or the result of the minting equipment that is not fine-tuned casing a machine error. Defective hubs[14] are the root cause of some doubling.

Collectors refer to doubled dies as DDO[15] - Doubled die obverse coins, DDR[16] – Doubled die reverse.

Mint Striking Errors

Collectors and organizations dedicated to collecting coins' regard mint striking errors as those created by the mint stamping process. Most of these coins command no significant value, especially those that have no date.

It is easy to get confused with an authentic doubled die and a mint striking error. Many coins in circulation appear doubled but the appearance of doubling is machine doubling and not actual die errors. Many of these coins appear on eBay as doubled dies and they are not, so the collector needs to be careful before bidding.

Striking a coin with debris causing an indentation on the coin or actual debris stamped into the coin is a mint striking error. Although these coins are not very valuable, the mint makes every effort to catch and destroy these coins before they make it to circulation.

Coins can become broad struck when the collar that is holding the coin in place in the stamping process is missing. A broad struck coin is larger in diameter than the intended result. Some broad struck coins can be of significant value.

Die Cap

A "die cap" error has the appearance of a soda bottle cap with some of the details inside the cap. Coins stuck in the die

---

[14] Hub – the tool used to create a die. It is the mirror image of a die in reverse.
[15] DDO – Double die obverse
[16] DDR – Double die reverse

16

and stamped several times are die cap errors.

Above-Die cap error 1999 Lincoln cent

Die Clash

A coin minted with traces of the reverse on the obverse or the opposite are "die clash" errors. Die clash errors result in the minting dies pressed together without a planchet between the dies. One die side is imprinted with the details of the other side of the die. In subsequent stampings of planchets, the coins minted contain some of the reverse or obverse on opposite sides of the coin.

Pictured above is a 1970 Lincoln cent with the pillars stamped on the obverse.

Off-Center

Mint striking errors also include the misaligned coins minted and escape detection. An off center coin is the result of the planchet not aligned correctly with the bottom die.

There are thousands of coins that have been collected for their off center mintage. An off-center coin is the result of the holder of the planchet becoming loose and then the stamping is off center. Below is a 1997 off center Lincoln cent.

The most valuable of these coins are those that have a full date. Most encapsulation services will only recognize off-center coins that are 5% or more misaligned.

There are also coins that contain multiple portraits stamped on a coin that has been stamped outside of the collar and somehow finds its way back into the stamping process to be stamped a second time.

Variations
Variations are not mint errors in the technical sense. Coins minted by creating hubs and dies that are not exactly the same result in dates that can be compared as large to small, wide to thin etc.

Die variations have resulted in the 1960 large and small dated Lincoln cent production, and the 1982 large and small dated series both in copper and copper-zinc cents minted. All of these coins are intentional coin variations by the mint and they are not coin errors.

Some die variations are very valuable and others command no value difference between the coin variations of the same date and mintmark. Coins minted with die variations increase in value by the rarity of the number of coins minted.

Early dated coins have the most variety. Dies produced coins until they were unusable. Many dies of an early year were used to make coins in later years. In the same year, the mint could have produced coins with several features that are on some of the coins minted that are not on others. For example, many early dated coins contain variations in the number of stars on the coin.

The value is based on the number of coins minted (or thought to be minted) with the lesser or greater number of a particular feature.

Coin Grading
Coin grading is subjective especially with mint state coins. Photographic coin guides that provide grading by denomination are helpful in determining the grade of a coin. We have added photographic grading to our coin guide of values, "US Coin Guide."

Carbon spotting does detract from a coin's value and the extent of the spotting many cause the coin classified as "corroded."

PCGS defines carbon spotting: *carbon spot*

A spot seen mainly on copper and gold coins, though also occasionally found on U.S. nickel coins (which are 75 percent copper) and silver coins (which are 10 percent copper). Carbon spots are brown to black spots of oxidation that range from minor to severe – some so large and far advanced that the coin is not graded because of environmental damage[17]

The coin above has severe carbon spotting reducing the value as an uncirculated sample.

Brilliant Uncirculated

PCGS defines BU as: A generic term applied to any coin that has not been in circulation. Sometimes applied to Lincoln cent coins with little "brilliance" left, coins not brilliant are simply Uncirculated. [18]

Many sellers are reserved with the use of "uncirculated" and use "brilliant uncirculated" as a reference for brown Lincoln cents. The proper identification is "uncirculated or MS__.

The major encapsulation services list coins as Red/Brown, Brown, or Red for Lincoln cents.

Choice Uncirculated

An Uncirculated coin grading MS-63 or MS-64. [19]

---

[17] PCGS carbon spot – from the PCGS web site

[18] PCS definition

[19] PCS definition

Chapter 2 – Large Cent Errors

Classifying coins of this era as an error coin or a variety coin is somewhat challenging since the mint often used dies that were distinctly different for the same year. For example, using a 1798 large cent die and modifying it to read 1799 is considered an over mint mark (OMM) by collectors and some of them are extremely valuable.

Dr. William Shelton[20] spent a life- time cataloging all of the large cent variances resulting in the "S" (Shelton) denotations for large cent variations. Many coin auctions list large cents as the date followed by an "S" classification number representing the variation of the coin. Another well-known collector Walter Breen[21] joined with William Shelton to develop the "R" scale[22] used to reveal the number of large cents for any particular date. In high- end auctions the Shelton-Breen scale[23] classifies large cents along with any encapsulation grading. In some books, there is no "R" scale reference to the low-7 and high-7 designation leaving R-7 to mean 4-12 coins and the R-8 interpreted as 1-3 coins. There are nine levels on the Sheldon-Breen rarity scale:

R-8: only one coin known to exist

R-7 High: A coin excessively rare; 2 to 3 exist

R-7 Low: An extremely rare coin with 4 to 12   known

R-6: A very rare coin with 13 to 30 known

R-5: 31 to 75 coins exist, classifying it as rare

R-4: A very scarce coin with 76 to 200 coins

R-3: With 201 to 500 estimated coins

R-2: A coin that is not common, with 501 to 1250 coins in existence

R-1: With at least 1251 coins remaining, this is a common coin.

Dr. Shelton was the pioneer in developing the foundation for the present day coin grading system. It was Dr. Shelton the designated coin grades by using a numbering system from 1 through 70 that has been converted to present day fair, about good, good, very good, fine, very fine, extra fine, about uncirculated, and Mint State (MS) grading systems of MS60

---

[20] William Shelton was one of the pioneers in developing coin-grading systems.

[21] Walter Breen- renowned collector and coin expert.

[22] R Scale – the number of coins minted.

[23] Shelton-Breen scale developed to classify the large cent rarities.

21

through MS70. It is impossible for the novice collector to grade any coin with an MS designation because there are no books available that can exactly describe the grading technique in recording the numbers of nicks, scratches, and surface blemishes that place an uncirculated coin in a specific MS grade. Sometimes the grading panel members at the encapsulation services cannot agree on a particular MS grade and the coin usually obtains the lower grade.

There are numerous examples of small and large date varieties, however, these are most likely the result of the die makers and perhaps should not be called errors but instead variations. So many variations of large cents by date exist that it would take the dedication of someone to author a book to reveal all of them. There were tall dates, short dates, wide letters, slanted dates, use of obverses and reverses of different dates, and variations in the design that require careful cataloging.

Pictured above is an 1807 over 1806 large cent

Some of the large cent error coins can command a remarkable amount of money at auction. An 1801 "three errors" coin (one stem, 1/1000, UNITED) sold on the internet for $275,000 in very good condition. The coin photographs presented well and the three errors clearly identified. A high-end collector desiring to put a collection of large cents together would most likely strive to obtain all of the variations and thus be willing to pay a lot of money to obtain one-coin error of every type.

Any of the rarer large cent error coins in about uncirculated or better conditions are likely to produce coin values well over $100,000. Research into past and present auctions has revealed a true rarity with these coins in the highest grades.

Variations and Errors

1797 reverse of 1797 stems (ANACS, G6, $184-$345) (NGC F, $862) (PCGS AU58, $5,462) (PCGS MS64, $16,100)

1797 reverse of 1797 no stems (NGC, G6, $322)

1797 reverse of 1795 (AG3, $488)

1798 second hairstyle (ANACS, G4, corroded, $56)

1799/1798 (PCGS Fair, $1,955) (PCGS G6, $12,650) (PCGS VG8, $8,050) (PCGS VG10, $10,925)

1799/1798 over date (PCGS VF35, $48,875)

1800/1798 over date (NGC G4, $207) (NGC VG10, $5,462) (NGC F15, $138-$875) (NGC VF25, $1,035-$1,995) (NCG AU58 cleaned, $4,025-$8,050) (ANACS MS65, $92,000)

1800/1799

1801 three errors (one stem, 1/1000, UNITED) (PCGS VG8, $529) (NGC VF30, $3,220-$3,737) (PCGS AU53, $14,950) (NGC AU58, $5,175) (NGC MS63, $138,000) 1801 1/100 over 1/1000 (PCGS VG10, $432) (NGC VF35, 1,380) (PCGS EF40, $2,530) (PCGS AU50, $3,594)

1803 Small Date Small Fraction (PCGS VF35 $547) (PCGS EF45, $1,610)

1803 Small Date Large Fraction (PCGS VG8, $173) (PCGS VF35 $633) (NGC AU50, $1,495) (NGC MS64, $16,100)

1804 broken dies re-strike (NGC MS64, $1,380) (PCGS MS66, $1,840)

1807 large 7/6 (NGC VG8, $2,990) (NGC VF30, $460-$1,495) (PCGS MS65, $86,250)

1807 small 7/ 6 (NGC VF25, $11,500-$27,500) (PCGS AU55, $161,000)

1807 small 7/6 blunt 1 (raw VF30, $3,960)

1811/1810 (ANACS AG3, $60-$66) (NGC G6, $250-$374) (ANACS F12, $286-$488) (PCGS VF35, $3,450) (PCGS EF 45, $3,200) (PCGS AU50, $6,600-$11,500)

23

1819/1818 (NGC EF45, $345) (ANACS AU50, $400-$546) (NGC MS64, $1,725)

1820/1819 (ANACS G6, $35) (ANACS VG8, $37) (NGC VF25, $149) (NGC AU55, $834)

1823/1822 none located

1839/1836 none located

1844/1881 (PCGS VG10, $125) (ANACS F12, $95) (ANACS VF20, $109-$161) (NGC EF45, $345) (PCGS AU55, $1,495) (PCGS MS64, $29,000)

1851/1881 (PCGS VF30, $126) (NGC EF45, $207-$373) (NGC AU58, $410) (PCGS MS65, $1,725-$4,312) (NGC MS66, $3,220-$5,750)

1855 slanted 5's (PR65, $715)

1856 slanted 5 (PCGS AU50, $126.50)

1857 small date (PCGS PR65, $8,050)

Chapter 3 – Small Cents

Flying Eagle 1856-1858

There are a few flying-eagle cent errors listed below. Because of the short mintage of the flying eagle cent, errors are limited to three years of mintage.

Pictured above is an 1856 flying eagle cent obverse and reverse

Variations and Errors

1857 struck on thin planchet (PCGS MS63, $3,800) 2016
1857 Doubled die obverse (PCGS MS65, $1,100)
1858 small date (NGC EF40, $84-$127) (PCGS MS64, $1,495)
1858 large date (NGC EF40, $138) (PCGS MS64, $1,092)
1858 8/7 (NGC VF30, $345) (ANACS EF40, $299) (PCGS AU50, $850-$1,100) (NGC AU58, $3,500) (NGC MS64, $10,350-$20,700) (NGC MS65, $27,600)

Ever wonder where all of the 1856 flying eagle cents went? Walter Breen, noted collector and well-respected coin expert published the following distribution of 1856 Flying Eagle Cents:

264 (or more) to Congressmen
200 to Representative S.D. Campbell
102 to Secretary of the Treasury James Guthrie
62 to Senators
4 to President Franklin Pierce
2 to the Mint Cabinet
Additional pieces were given to dignitaries and others"

Indian Cents 1859-1909

Pictured above is an 1859 Indian Cent

There are many types of errors for Indian cents encapsulated and sold at high-end auctions. It is nearly impossible to list and catalog all the errors that have resulted in missed-aligned dies, loose collars, and incorrect planchets.

Variations and Errors

1858 small letters DDR 3 (PCGS MS64, $1,380)

1859/1859 (NGC MS64, $1,150) 2017

1860 pointed bust (PCGS MS66, $12,650-$15,525)

1862 DDR (NGC MS63, $1,100) 2017

1864 L on the ribbon (PCGS EF45, $230-$276)

1864 without the L (NCG MS65, $299-$1,265 Red)

1864/64 (NGC G4, $35) 2015

1864/64 "L" on ribbon (NCG VG8, $94)

1865 DDO (PCGS AU55, $1,175) 2017

1865 fancy 5 (PCGS MS66, $12,650- $28,750)

1866 DDO Liberty (ANACS MS64, $2,250) 2017

1866 DDO (PCGS XF45, $459) 2017

1866 6 over 6 (ANACS G4, $32) 2015

1866 repunched 1 and 6 (NGC MS66, $1,725) 2017

1867/67 (IGC G6, $42) (PCGS F12, $253) (ANACS VG10, $144) (PCGS AU55, $700) (NGC MS65, $23,000-$24,380)

1868 DDO (NGC MS65 red, $920)

1869/69 repunched date (ANACS G4, $85) 2015

1870 shallow N in ONE (PCGS MS65, $4,200) 2017

1870 DDO (NGC G4, $51) (ANACS VG8, $90) 2015

1870 DDO and DDR (ANACS MS60, $431.25)

1870 DDR (ANACS VG8 $89) 2015

1871 shallow N in ONE (PCGS MS64, $3,400) 2017

1872 DDO (NGC MS65, $56) 2014

1872 shallow N in ONE (PCGS MS65, $5,100) 2017
1873 closed 3 (ANACS G4, $105) (NGC EF45, $172)
(PCGS MS66, $16,675)
1873 closed 3 DDO (ANACS VG8, $230) (ANACS VF35,
$184) (NGC MS63, $1,035)
1873 open 3 (H, NGC EF45, $138)
1873 double "LIBERTY" (NGC G4, $240) (PCGS VG10,
$632) (PCGS VF20, $833) (PCGS AU55, $3,565) (PCGS
MS65, $23,000-$69,000) (PCGS MS64, $32,200) 2015
1874 DDO (PCGS MS65, $1825) 2017
1877 stuck on a Venezuela one-centavo planchet (H,
NGC MS61, $21,850)
1880 DDO (PCGS MS65, $3500) 2017
1883 misplaced date (NGC MS66, $1175) 2017
**1886 Type I – feather pointing between IC rather than CA
letters.** (PCGS MS66, $8800) 2017
1886 Type 11 – feather pointing between CA (PCGS
PR65, $15275), (PCGS MS64, $7500) 2017
1887 DDO (PCGS AU53, $370) 2014
1888 8 over 7 (PCGS G4, $126.50) (PCGS VG30, $1800)
(PCGS VF30, $6,325) (PCGS EF45, $12,075-$12,600)
(PCGS MS63, $74500)
1891 DDO (PCGS MS64, $3200) 2017
1891 DDR – 001 (ANACS MS63, $184)
1894 misplaced date (PCGS MS64, (PCGS MS64, $1025)
2017
1894 double date (NGC VG10, $72) (PCGS MS65,
$10,500-$12,650)
1897 misplaced date (NGC MS63, $1525) 2017
1898 misplaced date (NGC MS65, $2000) 2017
1905 Indian cent struck on a quarter-eagle planchet
$253,000

Lincoln Cents 1909-date

Pictured above is a 1969-D Lincoln cent

Some mint errors are well known and others are documented but not as popular. Lincoln cent error coins have the highest number of encapsulation than any other coin series to date. The prices realized for Lincoln error coins are the highest among any other denomination, especially in grades of mint state.

The first year of mintage provided a variation in with the San Francisco mintage yielding an S over S mintage. The S over S mintage is not rare to the date itself since this coin sells for the same price as the 1909-S with no doubling. There are some examples of 1909 VDB coins with doubling on the obverse that have been discovered and encapsulated and they can sell from several hundred dollars to several thousand dollars depending upon the grade.

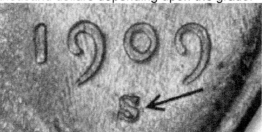

Pictured is a 1909-S/S coin

In 1922, the Denver mint used the dies on the obverse until the D no longer pressed into the coin resulting in a 1922 coins without the D. If there had been minting of the 1922 coin at the Philadelphia mint that year, it would have been a challenge to distinguish where the coins originated.

28

Pictured above is a 1922 Lincoln cent with no D

In 1922, four dies produced error coins for the 1922. The 1922-D full mint- mark, the 1922-D Weak D die set, the no D strong reverse, and the no D weak reverse. The 1922 no D coin is valued in a range of $300 in the lowest grade to over $5,000 in MS60 conditions. Some of these coins in MS64 and MS65 have sold between $40,000 and $50,000 at auction.

Pictured above a 1944-S Lincoln cent struck on a zinc planchet.

The Lincoln cent above is a 1944-S error coin minted on a zinc planchet. This coin sold for $373,750 on the Heritage auction site July 31, 2008.

There are some examples of 1943 and 1943-S minted Lincoln cents struck on bronze planchets out in the collecting world. Bronze 1943 samples sell in excess of $300,000. The most sought after Lincoln cent error coin has always been the 1955 doubled die. This is a true mint error coin with a very clear doubling of the date. At auction, a 1955 doubled die NGC MS-66 Red sold at Bowers & Merena Galleries "The Rarities Sale", July 31, 2002, Lot 63, illustrated, for $46,000[24]. There are thousands of 1955 doubled die cents sold at auction every day for collectors to obtain and enjoy and most at reasonable prices for the rarity of the coin.

Pictured above is the 1955 doubled die cent

Only two known examples of the 1958 double-die cent exist and both of them are PCGS MS65 specimens valued over $140,000. The doubling on the obverse of the 1958 DDO cent is on the motto "IN GOD WE TRUST" and the word "LIBERTY".

---

[24] Data from coin facts

Above is one of the rare 1958 doubled die cents

Not mint errors, but die varieties, the 1960 Lincoln cent series contains small dates and large dates. The small dated 1960 coins are generally valued at $6 for the 1960 small date in MS65 and $4 for the 1960-D small date in MS65 condition.

One of the most valuable more recent Lincoln cent double-die is the 1969-S. This coin can sell in excess of $50,000 in MS conditions since the number of these coins discovered has been extremely limited. The doubling in this coin is clear in LIBERTY, IN GOD WE TRUST, and the 1969-S date. Collectors need to be careful not to confuse machine doubling with the actual hub error minted coins. Machine doubling will show some letters and numbers to contain some flashing contributed from the pressing of the coin in the dies.

Pictured above is a 1969-S Lincoln cent doubled die. Note the extreme doubling of the word "LIBERTY."

The mint produced variations of the 1970-S Lincoln cent with a small date and a large dated version. The small dated version is valued between $50 and $100 depending upon the MS grade. The large date 1970-S coin is the standard issued coin, and it commands no extra value in circulated condition. The seven in the coin that serves as a reference point for differentiating the large version to the small version date. Drawing a line along the top of the date the seven, the small dated seven will be slightly below the rest of the date. It may be possible to locate the 1970-S low 7 cent in circulation since the two versions are difficult to distinguish at a glance.

Above is a photograph of a 1970-S small date 7. The 7 is just below the line of where the 9 and the 0 is touching.

Some proof variations occurred in 1979 were the filled S in some sets. These variations do not command any significant value and are common in proof sets.

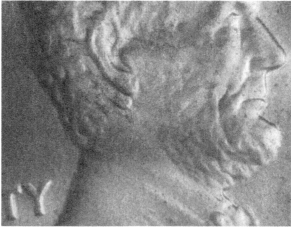

Above is a 1984 double ear Lincoln cent. The doubling of the ear is very clear.

Contrary to any belief, the 95% copper Lincoln cents did not end in 1959, it ended in 1982. The 1982 mintage is a mix of copper and copper clad coinage.

In 1982, the mint produced seven different Lincoln cents. With 95% copper content, the mint produced a 1982 small date, a 1982 large date, and a 1982-D large date. The composition of the Lincoln cent changed to 97% zinc and 3% copper with the minting of a 1982 large date, a 1982 small date, a 1982-D large date and a 1982-D small date. A collector aspiring to collect these variations can purchase the whole set for under $10 in uncirculated condition. The zinc in the coin shows by cutting a cent in half or removing the copper top layer of the cent.

In 1983, the mint released a percentage of coins with a doubling of the reverse. The doubling is the strongest in the word "ONE" but most of the double lettering on the reverse is legible by eyesight. These coins will yield between $400 and $750 in various MS grades.

A recent doubled die cent is the 1995. The doubling on these coins is not as apparent as other doubled die Lincoln cent coins. The doubling occurs in "LIBERTY" and "In GOD" with the doubling of liberty more pronounced. This coin sells for under $100 in mint state condition.

In 1997, some Lincoln cents appeared to have a double ear. The doubling occurs above the ear with hair doubled and with ear lobe. Some collectors dispute this coin as a doubled die cent and not noted in some coin guides. There is an example of a PCGS MS65 double ear coin that sold at auction for over $195.

Becoming an expect DDO and DDR numismatist has its rewards since there are collectors that are willing to pay $100 of more for these coins in encapsulation. Thousands of brilliant uncirculated rolls of Lincoln cents in the market can be searched for some of these DDO and DDR finds. Before sending any DDO or DDR coin to an encapsulation service, the collector should be sure the grade and the cost of encapsulation will yield a benefit.

A Lincoln cent obverse minted with the reverse of a dime sold auction for $138,000. Pictured below:

33

Collectors refer to this type of error as a mule.

No other coin series has as many error coins as the Lincoln cent series. The vast number of one-cent coins minted and the refurbishing of the dies have created thousands of RPM's. The number of errors and variations are numerous and new discoveries will continue as collectors search through their coins.
Lincoln errors include a vast number of samples minted on dime planchets.

Variations and Errors
1909 VDB DDO (PCGS MS63, $140-$175) (PCGS MS64, $145-$1,438) (PCGS MS65, $100-$4,888) (PCGS MS66, $747-$12,075)
1909 VDB DDR (ANACS MS64, $120) 2017
1909-S S over Horizontal S (ANACS VG10, $89) (ANACS F12, $160) (NGC VF35, $105-$184) (PCGS XF45, $160-$190), (NGC MS63, $299-$345) (NGC MS64, $518) (PCGS MS65, $1,006) (PCGS MS66, $2,070)
1910-S S/S (PCGS MS65, $1,725) 2017
1911-D D/D (PCGS VF25, $105) (PCGS XF40, $125) (PCGS AU58, $500) 2017
1911-S S/S (PCGS VF25, $100) (NGS AU55, $175) (ANACS MS61, $160) (ANACS MS63, $195) 2017
1912-S S/S (ANACS MS63, $200) 2017
1917 DDO (PCGS G04 $69-$185) (ANACS VG8, $140-$195), (ANACS VG10, $160) (PCGS F12 $144) (PCGS VF20, $280), (PCGS MS66, $25,300-$28,750)
1920 struck on an Argentina 10 cent (NGC AU55, $500) 2015
1922 no D or partial D (PCGS G6, $250) (ANACS VG8, $800) (PCGS AU55, $4,100) (PCGS MS63, $2,500-$14,000)

34

1925-S DDO (PCGS MS65, $1,125) (ANACS MS60, $375) 2017
1925-S S/S (PCGS F15, $50), (PCGS MS65, $1,100) 2016
1927 DDO (PCGD VF25, $99) (PCGS MS65, $525) 2017
1927 D/D (PCGS MS64, $660) 2014
1928-S Large S (PCGS MS63, $120) (PCGS MS64, $500-$700) 2017
1929-S S/S (PCGS MS65, $1, 060) 2017
1930-S S/S (PCGS MS64, $86-$125) (NGC MS66, $225) 2016
1932-D DDO (ANACS MS64, $115) 2017
1934 DDO (PCGS MS65, $950) 2017
1934-D/D (PCGS F12, $55), (PCGS MS65, $445) 2016
1935 DDO (PCGS MS63, $248). (NGC MS65, $440)
1936 DDO proof type I (ANACS VF35, $140) (ANACS XF40, $195), (PCGS MS63, $2,300) 2017
1936 proof type II DDO (ANACS PR62, $195), (PCGS MS66, $5,400-$5,750)
1936 DDO die 1 (PCGD F12, $90) (ANACS VF35, $144) (PCGS XF45, $95-$185) 2017
1936 DDO die 2 (PCGS VF30, $170) (PCGS XF45, $100-$185), (PCGS MS65, $3,500) (PCGS MS66, $11,500-$21,850)
1936 DDO die 3 (PCGS MS65, $1,700)
1936 DDO die 4 (ANACS MS65, $105) 2017
1936 DDR (ANACS MS66, $130) 2017
1938 DDR (ANACS MS65, $90) 2017
1938 D/D (NGC MS65, $40) (ANACS MS65, $21) 2014
1938-S Triple S (ANACS MS63, $95) (ANACS MS65, $21-$65) (NGC MS65, $72-$129) (NGC MS66, $39-$120) (NGC MS67, $100-$135) 2016
1938-S S/S (NGC VF25, $112) (PCGS MS64, $125) (ANACS MS65, $26-$300) (NGC MS66, $42-$225) (NGC MS67, $110-$260) 2016
1939-S S over S (MS65, $30) 2016
1939 DDO (ANACS MS64, $120) (PCGS MS66, $575-$960)
1940-D D/D (ANACS MS64, $23) 2014
1940-S S/S (ANACS MS64, $74) (ANACS MS65, $70) (ANACS MS66, $132)
1940-S Triple S (ANACS MS64, $26-$79) (ANACS MS66, $58)
1941 struck on a Panama cent (PCGS MS65, $4995) 2015

35

1941 DDO (PCGS VF20, $65) (NGC XF45, $150) (ANACS AU58, $175) (ANACS MS64, $160-$164) (PCGS MS65, $719-$6,325) (PCGS-NGC MS66, $5,175-$5,750)

1941-S DDR Class VI (ANACS MS65, $38-$41) (ANACS MS67, $100) 2017

1942 struck on a think brass planchet (ANACS VF30, $130) 2015

1942 struck on an Ecuador 10 centavos (NGC VF35, $1,880) 2015

1942 struck on a dime planchet (PCGS MS63, $6,200) (ANACS AU58, $11,750) 2015

1942 DDO (ANACS EF45, $38) (ANACS AU50, $19)

1942-D D/D (PCGS MS65, $300), (PCGS MS66, $460) 2015

1942-S DDO (PCGS MS64, $172.50) (PCGS MS65, $184) (PCGS MS66, $1,150)

1942-S S/S (ANACS EF45, $77) (ANACS MS65, $31) (NGC MS66, $288) (ANACS MS66, $38-$42) (ANACS MS67, $86-$225) 2016

1942-S DDR (ANACS MS63, $146)

1942-S Triple S (NGS MS64, $160) (NGC MS65, $345) (PCGS CAC MS66, $546) (NGC MS66, $288-$300) (NGC MS67, $432) 2016

1943 struck on a dime planchet (PCGS VF25, $1,750) (NGC AU50, $15,275) 2015

1943 overstruck on a Cuba 1 centavo (PCGS MS62, $38,200) 2015

1943 struck on bronze planchent (PCGS AU58, $218,500)

1943 struck on Curacao 25 cent planchet (NGC EF40, $14,950) (NGC AU58, $11,500)

1943 DDR (ANACS MS62, $30) 2017

1943 DDO (ANACS MS64, $135) (ANACS MS66, $195) 2017

1943 DDO/DDR (ANACS MS64, $85-$120) (NGC MS65, $80-$175) (ANACS MS66, $152-$185) 2017

1943-D D/D (PCGS MS65, $805- $2,530) (PCGS MS67, $4,500-$21,275)

1943-S DDO (PCGS MS65, $470), (PCGS MS66, $825) (PCGS MS67, 2,325) 2015

1943-S DDR minor doubling (ANACS MS61, $6) 2017

1943-S struck on a bronze planchet (PCGS VF35, $207,000)

1943-S struck on a dime planchet (PCGS AU50, $3,525) (PCGS AU55, $8,825-14,100) (PCGS AU58, $4,250) 2016

1944 zinc coated steel planchet (NGC AU50, $5,875) 2017

1944 struck on a brass planchet (NGC MS63, $425) 2015
1944 struck on a dime planchet (PCGS XF40, $3,050) 2015
1944 struck on a Netherlands 25 cent (PCGS MS63, $5,200-7,635) 2014
1944 struck on a Philippines 5 centavos (PCGS MS62, $6,400) 2015
1944-D struck on a dime planchet (PCGS MS65, $4400) 2015
1944-D D/D (ANACS MS60, $11), (PCGS MS64, $95) (PCGS MS65, $80-$125) (ANACS MS66, $200) (PCGS MS67, $2200) 2016
1944-D DDR (ANACS MS65, $184) 2017
1944-D with S located below the D (PCGS $29)
1944-D D/S (NGC VF30 $100) (NGC/PCGS XF45, $100-$155) (ANACS AU55/58, $140-$184) (NGC MS60, $250), (PCGS MS63, $125-$180) (PCGS MS66, $2,200- $16,100) (PCGS MS65, $5,100-$5,463)
1944-D struck on zinc coated steel planchet (NGC MS63, $115,000), (NGC AU50, $60,375)
1944-D on zinc planchet (NGC MS63, $115,000)
1944-S on zinc planchet (NGC MS66, $373,750)
1945 DDO (ANACS MS64, $120-$435) 2017
1945 struck on a Netherlands East Indies (NGC MS64, $765) 2015
1945 struck on an Ethiopia centavo (NGC MS62, $1,645) 2015
1945-D D/D (ANACS MS60, $25) 2014
1945-S struck on a dime planchet (NGC XF40, $560) 2015
1945-S struck over Netherlands East Indies (NGC AU58, $7,050) 2015
1945-S DDO (ANACS MS67, $167)
1945-S S/S (ANACS MS66, $150) 2016
1946-D D/D (ANACS MS64, $65) (NGC MS66, $75) 2016
1946-D struck on a dime planchet (ANACS AU50, $300) 2015
1946-S DDO (ANACS MS66, $31) (ANACS MS67, $165) 2017
1946-S S/D (PCGS XF45, $130) (NGC MS63, $150) (PCGS MS65, $977), (ANACS MS67, $425) 2017
1946-S S/S (ANACS MS63, $40) (ANACS MS64, $37) (ANACS MS66, $29) 2016
1947 DDO (PCGS MS64, $250), (PCGS MS66, $700-$1,300) 2014

1947-S S/S (ANACS MS64, $125) (ANACS MS65, $32 - $100) (ANACS MS66, $28) 2016
1948-S S/S DDO (ANACS MS65, $173)
1948-S S/S (ANACS MS66, $69) 2016
1949-D D/D (PCGS MS64, $75-$95) (PCGS MS65, $300) 2016
1949-S DDO (ANACS MS64, $120) (NGC MS65, $20-$125) (ANACS MS66, $145) 2016
1949-S S/S (ANACS MS65, $36-$75) 2016
1950-S S/S (PCGS MS65, $35-$41) (ANACS MS66, $21-$78) 2016
1951 DDO (PCGS PR64, $54-$95), (PCGS PR65, $90) (PCGS PR66, $235-$270)
1951-D DDO (PCGS MS63, $45) 2014
1951-D D/D (ANACS AU58, $12) (ANACS MS65, $69) 2016
1951-D Triple D (ANACS MS64, $75)
1952-D D/D (SEGS, MS65, $15) 2016
1951-D D/S (PCGS MS65, $118) (PCGS, MS66, $165-$300), NGC MS67, $2,350) 2014
1952-D D/S (PCGS MS64, $100-$160) (PCGS MS66, $525-$865) 2017
1952-S struck on a dime planchet (NGC XF45, $1,725) 2015
1952-S S/S (PCGS MS67, $117) 2016
1953 DDO (NGC MS65, $109) (PCGS PR66, $115-$267) (PCGS PR67, $125-$230)
1953 DDO (ANACS PR64, $90) 2017
1953 DDR (PCGS PR65, $150) (NGC PR66, $85) 2017
1953-D struck on a dime planchet (PCGS AU53, $920) 2015
1953-D D/D (PCGS MS65, $79-$85 2016
1953-S S/S (ANACS MS64, $85) (ANACS MS65, $28-$90) 2016
1954 D/D (PCGS MS64, $50-$65) (ANACS MS65, $69-$350) 2016
1954-D Triple D (ANACS MS65, $125) 2017
1954-S S/S (ANACS MS64, $14) (ANACS MS65, $28-$69) (ANACS MS66, $16-$22) 2016
1955 struck on Venezuela 25 cent (ANACS MS60, $1610) 2015
1955 DDO (PCGS AU58, $195) not double date 2015
1955 DDO (PCGS PR67, $95) 2017
1955 DDR (ANACS PR66, $90) 2017
1955 DDR and DDO (ANACS PR65, $25-$125)

1955 Doubled die (PCGS XF45, $700-$1,700) (PCGS AU58, $750-$2,100) (PCGS MS62, $1,700-2,400) (PCGS MS63, $2,000-$5,175) (PCGS MS64, $2,100-$5,400)
1955-D D/D (ANACS MS65, $22-$115) (ANACS MS66, $23-$120) 2016
1955-D D/S (PCGS MS65, $90) 2017
1955-D DDO (ANACS MS64, $42), (PCGS MS65, $146-$152) (ANACS MS64, $48-$92) (ANACS MS65, $42-$127) (NGC MS66, $60) (ANACS MS66, $25-$140) 2016
1955-S S/S (ANACS MS63, $48) (ANACS MS64, $48-$92) (ANACS MS65, $42-$127) (NGC MS66, $60) (ANACS MS66, $25) 2016
1955-S S/S/S (PCGS MS64, $32-$92) (ANACS MS65, $42-$127) (NGC MS66, $54-$165) (ANACS MS67, $79) 2016
1955-S Filled 5 (ANACS MS65, $42-$49) 2017
1956-D struck on Roosevelt dime (PCGS AU58, $2,590) 2015
1956-D D/S (ANACS MS64, $40-$95) (ANACS MS65, $155-$288) (PCGS MS66, $100) 2017
1956-D D/D (ANACS MS63, $90) (ANACS MS65, $35-$185), (PCGS MS66, $180-$260), (PCGS MS67, $1,293) 2016
1956-D Triple D (ANACS MS65, $59-$184)
1956-D D/D/S (ANACS MS65, $90-$120) (ANACS MS66, $95-$250) 2017
1957 struck on a 1957 dime (PCGS AU58, $3450) 2015
1957 struck on a dime Planchet (PCGS MS63, $825) 2015
1957-D struck on a dime Planchet (NGC XF40, $345) 2015
1957-D D/D (ANACS MS65, $29-$100) (ANACS MS66, $85) 2014
1957-D Triple D (ANACS MS65, $80)
1958 struck on a dime blank (NGC MS63, $940) 2015
1958 struck on a Cuba centavo (NGC AU58, $1575) 2015
1958-D D/D (ANACS MS64, $11) 2014
1958-D Triple D (PCGS MS65, $100) (ANACS MS66, $32) 2016
1959 DDO (ANACS MS62, $14), (PCGS MS64, $160) (PCGS MS65, $125-$200), (PCGS MS66, $825)
1959-D Triple D (ANACS MS63, $154) (PCGS MS65, $26-$184) (PCGS MS66, $30-$116)
1960 struck on a dime planchet (NGC MS60, $374) 2015
1960 Triple DDO (NGC PR65, $80), (PCGS PR66, $105-$345), (PCGS PR67, $165-$635)
1960 quadruple die obverse (NGC PR68, $575) 2017

1960 DDO Small over Large date (PCGS PR65, $299) (PCGS PR66, $276) (NGC PR67, $385), (PCGS PR68, $4,600)

1960 DDO Large over Small Date (PCGS PR66, $193), (PCGS PR67, $250-$400), (PCGS PR68, $603-$1,006), (PCGS PR69, $7,475)

1960-D DDO (ANACS MS64, $85) 2017

1960-D DDO Small over Large Date (PCGS PR66, $276) 2014

1960-D DDO Large over Small Date (NGC PR64, $109) (NGC PR65, $138-$219) (NGC PR66, $161-253) (NGC PR67, $253-483)

1960-D D/D Small over Large Date (PCGS MS64, $125-$155) (PCGS MS65, $130-$376) 2016

1960-D D/D Large over Small Date (PCGS MS64, $9), (PCGS MS66, $676) 2016

1961 struck on a dime planchet (NGC MS63, $1,700) 2015

1961-D struck on a 1960-D small date (PCGS AU58, $4,600) 2016

1961-D D/D (ANACS MS65, $90-$105) 2014

1961-D over Horizontal D (PCGS MS64, $25-$50) (ANACS MS65, $94) 2016

1962 struck on a Philippine 10 centavo (NGC MS65, $575) 2015

1962 struck on a dime planchet (NGC MS65, $3825) 2015

1962 ANACS Proof DDO

1963-D DDO (PCGS MS64, $38) 2011

1964 struck on a dime planchet (ANACS MS64, $5,750) 2015

1964 SMS (PCGS MS67, $11,500)

1964 DDO (ANACS MS65, $115) 2014

1964 DDR (NGC MS62, $34), (ANACS MS63, $105) (ANACS MS64, $125-$150) (PCGS MS65, $109-$275), (PCGS MS66, $376)

1964-D struck on a dime planchet (NGC MS64, $597) 2015

1965 struck on a clad dime planchet (PCGS MS64, $550) 2015

1965 struck on a 1965 dime (NGC MS65, $1,765) 2015

1966 DDO (PCGS AU58, $25)

1966 staple embedded (NGC MS62, $1150) 2015

1966 struck on a dime planchet (PCGS MS65, $382) 2015

1967 DDO (NGC MS60, $47) 2015

1967 struck on a dime planchet (PCGS AU58, $520) 2015

1968 Struck on a Canadian dime planchet (ANACS MS62, $400) 2015

1968-D D/D (NGC MS65, $38) (PCGS MS65, $165) 2016

1968-S DDR (PCGS PR68, $525) 2017

1968-S DDO (ANACS MS64, $65-$90) (PCGS MS65, $90) (PCGS MS66, $185), (PCGS PR67, $195-$260) 2017

1968-S struck on a dime planchet (PCGS MS64, $299) 2015

1969 struck on a Canadian dime planchet (NGC MS62, $3,820) 2015

1969 double struck on a dime (NGC MS62, $3,820) 2015

1969-D struck on a dime planchet (NGC MS60, $275) 2015

1969-S doubled die obverse (PCGS MS63, $57,500-$86,250), (PCGS MS64, 126,500)

1970 struck on a dime planchet (ANACS MS64, $368) 2015

1970-S large date struck on dime planchet (PCGS PR64, $2,990) 2015

1970-S large date DDO (PCGS PR63, $28) light version

1970-S large date triple struck (NGC $470) 2017

1970-S DDO small date (PCGS PR68, $800-$2,050) 2017

1970-S DDO large date (PCGS MS63, $5,750) (PCGS MS64, $10,500) (PCGS MS65, $5,462)

1970-S S/S (ANACS MS63, $74) (ANACS MS64, $26- $38) 2016

1970-S S/S proof (NGC PR65, $250) 2017

1970-S triple die obverse proof (ANACS PR64, $110) 2017

1971 DDO (ANACS MS63, $160-$185) (PCGS MS64, $141-$634) (PCGS MS65, $1,725) (PCGS MS66, $10,500)

1971-D struck on a dime planchet (PCGS MS62, $860) 2015

1971-S DDO (PCGS PR64, $125-$135) (NGC PR65, $95-$150), (NGC PR66, $100-$250), (NGC PR67, $603-$805)

1971-S S/S
(PCGS MS64, $42-$427) (PCGS MS65, $26-$431) (PCGS MS67, $5,400-$5,750)

1972 72/72 (ANACS MS63, $140-$175) (ANACS MS64, $59-$460) (ANACS MS65, $125-$662) (PCGS MS66, $718-$1,122) (NGC MS67, $2,245)

1972-D/D (ANACS MS66, $27) 2016

1972-S DDO (ANACS PR64, $155) (NGC PR66, $230) 2017

1974 struck on a dime planchet (NGC MS66, $382) 2015

1975 struck on a dime planchet (NGC MS61, $305) 2015

1977 struck on a 1977 dime (NGC MS67, $2,100) 2015

1977 struck on a dime planchet (ANACS MS64, $415) 2015

1978 struck on a dime planchet (ANACS MS62, $665) 2015
1979-D Lincoln cent struck on a dime planchet (ANACS MS65, $575) 2015
1979-S Clear S (PCGS PR70, $1,400) 2017
1980 DDO (PCGS MS63, $185), (PCGS MS64, $125-$280), (PCGS MS65, $235-$250) 2016
1980 struck on a dime planchet (PCGS MS64, $765) 2015
1980-D D/S (PCGS MS65, $125) (PCGS MS66, $230-$400) 2017
1980-D struck on a dime planchet (NGC MS63, $260) 2015
1981 struck on a 198x dime (PCGS MS66, $1,050) 2015
1981-D struck on a dime planchet (NGC MS64, $300) 2015
1981-S Type 1 filled S (PCGS PR70, $125) 2017
1981-S Type 2 clear S (PCGS PR69, $100-$185) 2017
1982 large date stuck in dime planchet (NGC MS65, $575) 2015
1982 small date stuck in dime planchet (PCGS MS64, $431) 2015
1982 DDO large date die 2 (ANACS MS65, $21)
1982 DDO small date copper
1982 DDO large date copper
1982-D DDO larger date copper
1982-D DDO small date zinc/copper plated
1982-D DDO small date zinc/copper plated
1982-D DOO large date zinc/copper plated
1982-D DDO larger date zinc/copper plated
1983 struck on an un-plated planchet (NGC MS66, $282) 2015
1983 struck on a copper planchet (PCGS AU55, $16,500) 2014
1983 DDO (NGC MS64, $42-$200), (ANACS MS65, $150-$184), (PCGS MS66, $250-$650) (PCGS MS67, $2,350)
1983 DDR (PCGS MS63, $120-$195), (PCGS MS64, $180-$245) (NGC MS68, $3,220)
1984 stuck on a dime planchet (PCGS MS62, $600) 2015
1984 DDO double ear (ANACS MS62, $51) (NGC MS63, $115-$125) (ANACS MS63, $140) (PCGS MS64, $125-$184) (PCGS MS65, $150-$245) (PCGS MS66, $130-$495) (PCGS MS67, $250-$805) (PCGS MS68, $2,250)
1984-D D/D (ANACS MS64, $188) 2017
1985 struck on a dime planchet (PCGS MS65, $765) 2015
1986 struck on a dime planchet (ANACS MS61, $225) 2015
1987 struck on a dime planchet (PCGS MS65, $940) 2015
1988 struck on a dime planchet (NGC MS64, $390) 2015

1989 struck on a dime planchet (PCGS MS66, $450) 2015
1989 struck on a 1988 dime (NGC MS65, $2,115) 2015
1990 struck on a dime planchet (NGC MS64, $650) 2015
1990 no S proof (PCGS PR66, $5,400-$5,750)
1991 struck on a dime planchet (ANACS MS65, $881) 2015
1992-D close AM (PCGS AU58, $2,115) 2017
1992 struck on a 1992 dime planchet (ANACS MS63, $1,438) 2015
1993 struck on a dime planchet (NGC MS66, $460) 2015
1994 struck on a dime planchet (PCGS MS66, $700) 2015
1994 DDR (NGC MS64, $79-$185) (PCGS MS65, $105-$990)
1995 struck on a dime planchet (PCGS MS64, $882) 2015
1995 DDO (PCGS MS67, $69-$138) (PCGS MS68, $79-$250)
1995-D DDO (PCGS MS65, $558) 2017
1996 DDO (NGC MS61, $89) 2015
1996-D struck on a zinc planchet (PCGS MS64, $130) 2015
1997 struck on a dime planchet (PCGS MS63, $650) 2015
1997 double ear (ANACS MS65, $105) (PCGS MS65, $152-$196)
1998-S close AM (NGC MS66, $125) 2017
1998-S close AM (PCGS PR69, $235-$1,400) 2017
1998 struck on dime planchet (PCGS MS67, $430) 2015
1998 struck on a 1998 dime (NGC MS65, $825) 2015
1999-S close AM (PCGS PR65, $105) (PCGS PR67, $100-$170) (PCGS PR68, $160-$200), (PCGS PR69, $125-$250) 2017
1999 stuck on a dime planchet (PCGS MS65, $680) 2015
1999 struck on a 1999 dime (NGC MS67, $950) 2015
2000 struck on 2000 dime planchet (NGC MS66, $805) 2015
2000 struck on a dime planchet (NGC MS67, $650) 2015
2001 struck on a Sacagawea dollar (PCGS MS66, $32,250) 2015
2001 struck on a dime planchet (PCGS MS64, $650) 2015
2001 struck on a 2000 dime (NGC MS63, $1,645) 2015
2006 DDO (PCGS MS65, $50) 2016
2009 formative years – rail splitter with a 6th finger (ANACS MS66, $95)
2014 DDO (PCGS MS64, $150) 2016

Chapter 4– Two Cent 1864-1873

There are very few coin errors in the market place concerning two-cent pieces.

Pictured above is an 1864 two-cent piece

Variations and Errors

1864 large motto (NGC AU58, $978) (NGC MS65, $345-$1,624) (PCGS MS66, $3,047-$3,738)

1864 large motto rotated dies (NGC AU50, $99)

1864 small motto (PCGS MS64 $2,300-$3,000) (NGC MS65, $852-$21,850) (PCGS MS66, $32,200)

1867 DDO (ANACS VG10, $60) (ANACS VF30, $127) (NGC MS62, $2,530) (ANACS AU50, $632.50) (PCGS MS64, $6,175)

Chapter 5– Three Cent 1851-1873

The three-cent piece was another one of the US Mint's short-lived series.

The content of silver in these coins was 75% with 25% copper. Production of these coins reduced the shortage of coins created by the gold rush in California. The lack of popularity rendered the coin to discontinuation and replaced by the three-cent–nickel.

In 1863, coins resulted in using dies of the 1862 version causing the three striking over the two. This error date is restricted to the proof issues in 1863.

Any date in this series that is in MS65 condition or higher is likely to realize in excess of $10,000 regardless of containing an error or not.

Pictured above is an 1856 three cent silver

The difficulty with collecting this series would be to locate the dates from 1863 through 1873. In good condition, these coins will sell between $250 and $300.

Variations and Errors

1862 2 over 1 (PCGS XF45, $156) (PCGS MS64, $13,800) (PCGS MS66, $1,500-$4,448) (NGC MS67, $3,000-$3,450)
1883 3 over 2 (NGC PR66, $6,900- $8,944) (NGC PR67, $13,225)

Chapter 6 – Three-Cent Nickel 1865-1889

Series completion requires devoting time to look for the coins for a collection. A few dates would set a collector back some cash. The 1883, 1884, 1885, 1886, and 1887 dates are the rarest in the collection with coin values starting between $200 and $300 in good condition.

The only date that contains a variation is the 1873. The mint produced one version with a closed three and another with a normal open three.

Pictured above is an 1885 three-cent nickel

Although this coin appears to be silver, it is not. The composition of this coin is 75% copper and 25% nickel. The coins are nick named "three cent nickel" verses a three-cent piece.

Variations and Errors
1873 open 3 (PCGS MS65, $3,750-$4,025)
1873 closed 3 (PCGS MS65, $2,700) (PCGS MS66, $2,700-$3,680) (NGC PR67, $3,300-$4,300)

Chapter 7 – Nickels 1866 to date

The first nickel minted in 1866 started the series and the nickel was on its way to become a yearly mint release to this day. The nickel permanently replaced the three-cent piece after 1889.

The Shield Nickel 1866-1883

Even though the US Mint was issuing three-cent pieces, it was not enough to satisfy the demand for coinage in circulation. The first nickel minted contained rays that circled the large five on the coin. In 1867, this version and a version of the nickel without the rays became part of the mintage. The version of the nickel with the rays ended after 1867. The 1867 version with the rays is more valuable than the version without the rays especially in grades of MS.

Variations and Errors

1868 DDR (NGC MS64, $547) 2015
1868 DDO (PCGS Genuine, $127) 2015
1870 DDR (PCGS XF45, $150) 2015
1870/70 DDO (NGC VF, $224) 2015
1872 DDO (ANACS PR62, $299) 2015
1872 CAMEO (PCGS PR66, $1265) 2015
1873 DDO (PCGS Genuine, $280) 2015
1873 DDO closed 3 (NGC MS62, $650) 2015
1874 DDO (NGC MS63, $355) 2015
1875 DDO (ANACS AU55, $140) 2015
1879 over 8 (PCGS PR66, $900) 2017

Shield nickels in the lowest conditions are affordable with prices between $15 and $50 each with a few exceptions. The keys to this collection are the 1879, 1880 and the 1881 coins which start at values of $250 in good condition and escalate into the $500 range for extra fine.

Pictured above is an 1877 nickel

It appears that there are very few error coins in this series but it does not mean that one will appear in the future.

The Liberty Head Nickel 1883-1913

Above is an 1897 Liberty nickel

The metal content of the nickel remained unchanged with the mintage of the liberty head, just a total redesign of the coin to show liberty on the front of the coin and the famous "V" on the reverse. This coin fell in line with most of the coinage of the day that placed liberty on the front of coins. Many collectors refer to this nickel as the "V Nickel." The first mintage of the coin did not denote cents on the coin, which could have left the "V" open for interpretation. The mint quickly modified the design to include the word "cents" on the first year of issuance in 1883.

Today the 1883 with "cents" rises in value significantly above the issuance without the word.

No mint errors are widely publicized in this series.

The rarest coin in the series is the 1913 "V" nickel, selling in excess of $4 million.

48

Pictured above is the rarest known nickel

The keys to this collection are the 1885 with a value over $275 in good condition and the 1912-S with a value of $75 in good condition excelling to over $500 in extra fine condition. There are proof-coins minted that can bring over $10,000 at auction.

We found that a complete set of liberty nickels sold for $14,500 in MS64 condition at auction. This is a bargain for this set since individually purchased coins of the same grade would far exceed the $14,500.

The Buffalo Nickel 1913-1938

Above is a 1923 Buffalo nickel

The design of the buffalo nickel ended the rein of liberty on US coinage for nickels. The nickel design featured an American Indian on the front of the coin and a buffalo on the reverse of the coin.

The inherent problem with the buffalo nickel design was that the date was the highest point on the obverse causing it to wear off completely in coins that would otherwise grade good or very good. On the reverse of the coin, the horn of the buffalo became a focal point for coin grading. A coin with no horn is in good condition. A coin graded in very good condition revealed a partial horn. A grade of fine would show ¾ of the horn. A grade of very fine would entail showing a full horn with wear at the tip of the horn. A grade of extra fine would require that the horn be fully outlined with moderate wear.

The best know error coin in the buffalo nickel series is the three-legged buffalo dated 1937-D. The refurbishing the die used to produce the coin continued until the leg wore off the die.

Pictured above is a 1937-D 3-legged buffalo

As the picture above reveals, part of the front leg of the buffalo was missing. An MS66 encapsulated coin can sell at auction for over $80,000. The average value for a 1937-D 3-leg buffalo in good condition is around $165. The price steadily rises until the value of the coin exceeds $400 in extra fine condition.

The mint produced two versions of the 1913 buffalo nickel intentionally. One version portrays the buffalo on a mound and the second version shows the buffalo on flat ground. Collectors refer to these coins as type one and type two versions with mintages from Philadelphia, Denver, and San Francisco. Both versions are easy to recognize since there is a distinct difference between the mound and flat ground issues.

Buffalo nickel type 2 flat ground.

1918-8 over seven

The 1918/17 dated coins in MS condition of MS64 or better can sell in excess of $250,000.

As with many of the error coins in MS conditions, the prices realized are dependent upon the auction site and the number of bidders who are seeking that particular coin. This may explain the wide variances in at auction prices for some error coins.

Variations and Errors
1913 buffalo on mound (PCGS MS64, $115)
1913 buffalo on flat ground (PCGS MS64, $115)
1913-D buffalo on mound
1913-D buffalo on flat ground (NGC MS65, $126-$977)
1913-S buffalo on mound (PCGS MS64, $230-$250)

1913-S buffalo on flat ground (PCGS MS64, $1,169)
1914 4/3 (PCGS MS64, $12,777) (PCGS MS65, $18,400)
1915-S S/S (PCGS G6, $65) (PCGS F15, $470) (PCGS XF40, $258) (PCGS AU58, $1.8 K) 2017
1916 DDO (NGC Fine, $977-$4,800) (PCGS VF25, $5,885) (PCGS EF45, $17,825-$22,425) (PCGS MS64, $184,000-$264,500)
1917-S Two Feathers (ANACS G6, $24) (ANACS F15, $65) (PCGS VF25, $211) (PCGS XF45, $3,290) 2017
1917 DDR (PCGS MS64, $10,925) 2015
1917-D 3.5 leg (PCGS G6, $74-$219) (PCGS VG8, $74-$633) (PCGS VF 35, $253) 2017
1918 DDR (PCGS VG10, $235) 2015
1918-D 8/7 (ANACS/PCGS Good, $690-$978) (PCGS VF30, $4,887-$6,612) (PCGS EF45, $4,887-$7,475) (NGC AU53, $13,800) (NGC MS62, $47,000) (PCGS MS64, $69,000-$74,000) 2017
1920 struck on a one-cent planchet (NGC AU55, $4,945)
1926-S (NGC MS65, $43,700)
 (PCGS MS65, $155,000-$264,000)
1921-S Two Feathers (PCGS VG10, $126) (PCGS F12, $646) 2017
1926-D Two Feathers (PCGS VF25, 101) 2017
1927–S DDO (PCGS VF35, $94) 2017
1930 DDO (PCGS MS64, $165-$550) 2015
1930 DDR (PCGS AU50, $115) (NGC MS65, $750 -2,500) 2015/17
1930-S S/S (ANACS MS62, $431)
1934 DDO (ANACS AU50, $315) 2015
1935 DDR (NGC F12, $39) (PCGS VF20, $150) (PCGS VF25, $276) (PCGS MS65, $25,300)
1936 DDO die 1(ANACS MS63, $110) 2015
1936-D three ½ legs (PCGS not graded damaged, $488)
1936-S S/S (ANACS MS62, $156) 2017
1937-D three legged (NGC VF20, $604-$650) (NGC EF45, $750- $776) (NGC AU55, $1,000-$1,150) (PCGS MS64, $8,050) (PCGS MS66, $86,250)
1938-D D/D (NGC AU58, $38) (PCGS MS66, $54-$185)
1938-D D/S (NGC MS66, $95-$175)
1938-D D/S over mint-marked.

The Jefferson Nickel 1938-date
In 1938, the first Jefferson nickel minted in 1938 along with the last issue of the Buffalo nickel. Since the Buffalo nickel

minting continued, the Jefferson 1938 series was limited in production. This made the 1938-D and the 1938-S Jefferson nickels semi-key coins to the collection. By the 1960's the 38-D and S coins were rare in circulation and could not be easily located.

The keys to the Jefferson nickel collection are the 1939-D and 1950-D coins but some of the other dates actually are rarer and more valuable in the MS conditions.

Pictured above is 1942-D/D Jefferson nickel

Since 1981, it appears that the mint has done a good job of ensuring that no error coins result in any significant amount. As with all of these types of error coins, the value is what someone is willing to pay.

Below is a listing of Jefferson nickel error coins that have sold at well-known and high-end auctions. There is a wide deviation in prices paid for the same grade and collectors need to be wary of over paying.

Coins denoted FS are Full Step Nickels. Many full step nickels with errors sell with no significance verses non-full step nickels.

Variations and Errors
1938 DDO (PCGS MS64FS, $500) 2014
1938 quadrupled DDO (PCGS MS64, $115-$140) (PCGS MS66, $200-$400) 2017
1938 D/D (PCGS MS65, $125) 2016
1938-D/S (PCGS MS67, $1,495) 2017
1939 DDO and DDR (ANACS MS 65, $58) 2015
1939 DDR ((ANACS AU50, $130) (ANACS MS65, $58) 2015
1939 reverse of 1938 (PCGS MS67 FS, $1,645) (PCGS PR68, $2,990- $11,000)
1939 reverse of 1938 DDR (ANACS AU58, $65) (ANACS MS60, $120) 2015

1939 reverse of 1940 (PCGS PR66 Cameo, $2,875-$8,625) (PCGS PR66, $525) (PCGS PR67 FS, $1,300-$3,000)
1939 Doubled Monticello (PCGS VF30, $85-$140) (PCGS XF40, $55-$120) (PCGS AU58, $160-$350) (PCGS MS63, $240) (PCGS MS64, $220-$1,050) (PCGS MS65, $385-$2,550) (PCGS MS65 FS, $11,100) (PCGS MS66, $525-$2,000) (PCGS MS66 FS, $1,100-$6,900) (PCGS MS67, $1,900-$3,100) (PCGS MS67 FS, $1,880-$20,560)
1939 quadrupled reverse (PCGS MS65, $350) (PCGS MS66, $325-$940) (PCGS MS67, $3,000) 2017
1939 DDO (ANACS AU58, $125) (ANACS, MS65, $58-$200) 2014
1939-D reverse of 1938 (PCGS MS66 FS, $4,715-$7,425) (PCGS MS67 FS, $1,100) (PCGS PR68, $12,925)
1939-D reverse of 1938 DDO (PCGS MS67, $345-$500) (PCGS MS67 FS, $620-$910) 2015
1939-D reverse of 1940 (PCGS MS66 FS, $565-$3,593) (PCGS MS67, $7,475) (PCGS MS67 FS, $2,500-$2,800)
1939-S reverse of 1938 (PCGS MS65, $20-$50) (PCGS MS65 FS, $250-$525) (PCGS MS66, $40-$250) (PCGS MS66 FS, $350-$8,050) (PCGS MS67, $400-$1,500)
1939-S reverse of 1940 (PCGS MS65 FS, $515) (PCGS MS66 full steps, $2,875)
1939-S quadruple DDO (PCGS MS67, $1055) 2017
1940 reverse of 1938 (ANACS PR62, $30-$65) (ANACS PR63, $85-$115) (PCGS PR64, $120-$400) (PCGS PR65, $210-$445) (PCGS PR66 Cameo, $8,625) (PCGS PR66, $420-$1,325) (PCGS PR67, $820-$2,800) (PCGS PR68, $9,775-$28,750) 2017
1940-D DDR (ANACS, MS65 $115)
1940-S S/S (PCGS MS65 FS, $350) (NGC MS66, $130)
1941 struck on a Lincoln cent (NGC VF20, $940) 2015
1941-D D/D (PCGS MS65, $1,125) 2017
1941-S Large S (PCGS MS65, $75) (PCGS MS65 FS, $330) 2014/2017
1942 struck on silver planchet (PCGS G6, $9,987) 2017
1942 type one DDO (ANACS MS63, $120) (PCGS MS65, $690) (PCGS MS66 FS, $3,000) 2014
1942 DDO (NGC MS64, $92-$160) (PCGS MS65, $375) (PCGS MS65 FS, $500) (PCGS MS66, $775) 2015
1942-D D over horizontal D (PCGS F12, $50) (PCGS VF20, $75-$95) (PCGS XF45, $70-$525) (PCGS AU55, $275-$1,645) (PCGS MS60, $1,600) (PCGS MS63, $3,000-

$4,400) (PCGS MS63 FS, $8,050) (PCGS MS64, $1,250-$8,625) (PCGS MS64 full steps, $5,400-$32,200) (PCGS MS65, $4,400-$14,950) (PCGS MS65 FS, $1,265-$30,550) (PCGS MS66, $3,500-$17,000) (PCGS MS66 FS, $1,200-$31,725)[25]

1942-S DDO (ANACS MS65, $30-$70) 2017

1943-P DDO (ANACS MS64, $135-$405) (PCGS MS65, $80-$865) (PCGS MS65 FS, $920-$1,200) (PCGS MS66 FS, $260-$2,350 (PCGS MS66, $365-1,050) (PCGS MS66 FS, $1,500-$2,070) (PCGS MS67, $880-$1,300) (PCGS MS67 FS, $2,990-$11,500) 2017

1943-P 3 over 2 (PCGS AU55, $200-$250) (PCGS MS63, $200-$335) (PCGS MS64, $200-$840) (PCGS MS64 FS, $490-$800) (PCGS MS65, $330-$1,000) (PCGS MS65 FS, $760-$2,000) (PCGS MS66, $500-$3,800) (PCGS MS66 FS, $2,100-$2,300) (PCGS MS67, $1,450-$4,200) (PCGS MS67 FS, $2,530-$16,675) (PCGS MS68, $3,400-$4,300)

1943-P 3/2 DDO (PCGS MS66 FS, $1,000-$2,600) (PCGS MS67, $5,600-$6,500) 2017

1943-P DDO (PCGS AU50, $60) (PCGS AU58, $185) (PCGS MS64, $140-$400) (PCGS MS65, $80-$635) (PCGS MS65 FS, $900-$965) (PCGS MS66, $260-$1,550) (PCGS MS66 FS, $960-$2,350) (PCGS MS67, $750-$11,500)

1943-D struck on copper planchet (ANACS MS64, $1,850) 2017

1944-P struck on copper nickel planchet (NGC VF30, $6,900)

1944-D D/D (PCGS MS66, $305)

1945-P DDR (PCGS (PCGS MS63, $95-$230) (PCGS MS64, $30-$375) (NGC MS64 FS, $160) (ANACS MS65, $200-$1,450) (PCGS MS65 FS, $75-$5,200) (PCGS MS66, $150-$5,200) (PCGS MS66 FS, 1600-$14,100) (PCGS MS67, $1,800-$3,800)

1945-P Triple P (PCGS MS65 FS, $1300) (PCGS MS65, $225-$950) (PCGS MS66, $1175-$2600) (NGC MS67, $1300) 2017

1945-P triple die reverse (PCGS MS66, $1,495) 2017

1946-D D over horizontal D (PCGS AU55, $165) (PCGS MS64, $1,350-$2,000) (NGC MS65, $1,495) (PCGS MS65 FS, $1,250-$1,400) (PCGS MS66, $1,350-$5,600) (PCGS MS66 FS, $2,100-$3,700) 2017

---

[25] The highest prices are paid for coins with full steps.

1946-D D over D (PCGS MS64, $1,265-$3,220) (PCGS MS65, $1,725-$3,000) (PCGS MS66 FS, $1,650-$11,500)
1946-D D over inverted D (PCGS MS66 FS, $1,235-$1,525) PCGS MS67, $1,300) 2017
1946-S DDO ((PCGS MS64, $280-$1,050) (PCGS MS65, $1,000-$2,875) (PCGS MS66, $1,175)
1949-D D/S (PCGS MS64, $165-$350) (PCGS MS65, $280-$8,050) (PCGS MS66, $480-$1,300) (PCGS MS66 FS, $975-$8,050) (PCGS MS67, $1,250-$2,600) (PCGS MS67 FS, $32,900)
1951 DDO (PCGS PR66, $80-$150) (NGC PR67, $115-$400) (NGC PR68, $440-$6,450) (NGC PR69, $3,525) 2014
1952 re-engraved obverse (PCGS PR66, $110)
1953 DDO (PCGS PR65, $21) (PCGS PR66 Cameo, $60) (PCGS PR67, $90-$310) (PCGS PR67 Cameo, $200) (PCGS PR68, $650) (NGC PR68 Cameo, $500-$6,450) (NGC PR69, $630-$4,700) 2014
1953-D D over inverted D (ANACS MS63, $125) (ANACS MS64, $225) (PCGS MS65, $250)
1954-S S/D (PCGS MS64, $35-$250) (PCGS MS65, $50-$575) (PCGS MS66, $330-$3,450)
1955 triple die reverse (PCGS PR67, $150) (NGC PR68, $200-$330)
1955-D D/S (PCGS MS64, $30-$1,500) (PCGS MS65, $50-$475) (PCGS MS66, $2,800-$3,737)
1956 DDO (NGC PR66, $40) (PCGS PR67, $75-$155) (PCGS PR68, $40-$325)
1956 triple die reverse (PCGS MS65, $160)
1956 quadruple DDR (ANACS MS64, $140)
1957 quadruple DDO (PCGS PR67, $220)
1957 quadruple DDR (PCGS MS65, $140)
1960 DDR (ANACS PR66, $30) 2017
1960 quadruple DDR (PCGS PR65, $130-$285) (PCGS PR66, $365-$380) (PCGS PR67, $650-$1,000) 2017
1961 DDR (ANACS MS65 FS, $130) 2016
1961 triple die reverse (PCGS PR66, $415) (PCGS PR67, $425)
1964-D D/D (PCGS MS65, $1,750-$2,800) 2017
1968-S S/S (PCGS PR67, $400) 2017
1971 proof missing S (PCGS PR69, $2,990-$4,485)
1977 struck on a 1976 cent (NGC MS64, $4,600) 2015
1990-S DDO (NGC PR69, $400-$920) (NGC PR69, $350-$400) 2014

1998 struck three times (NGC MS64, $950) 2014
2004-P DDR (NGC, MS64, $25-$125)
2004-P peace metal DDO (NGC MS64, $50-$100) 2014
2005-D speared bison (PCGS MS64, $25-$875) (PCGS MS65, $200) (PCGS MS66, $500-$1,200)
2005-D speared bison with detached leg (ANACS MS65, $100)
2005-D bison with detached leg (ANACS MS64, $20-$195)

57

Chapter 8 – Half Dimes 1794-1873

It is ironic that the mint produced a ½ dime while nickels were minted starting in 1866. The half-dime series provides many coins with variations. The mint changed the half dime design several times to include the flowing hair design dated 1794 to 1795. The draped bust with a small eagle dated 1796 to 1797 was minted. The draped bust dime mintage included a large eagle dated 1800 through 1805, the liberty cap dime from 1829 through 1837, a seated liberty dime from 1837 through 1859, and a final design dated 1860 through 1873 with the addition of the United States of America on the obverse.

Damaged, plugged, bent, holed, scratched, and/or cleaned coins are still valued in the hundreds for some dates.

Pictured above is an 1837 ½ dime. Draped bust design

Variations and Errors

1796 6/5 (NGC XF45, $9,800) (PCGS AU58, $25,900) (PCGS MS62, $27,600) (PCGS MS63, $28,200) (PCGS MS66, $172,500-$345,000)

1796 LIKERTY (PCGS F15, $4,150) (PCGS VF20, $1,550-$3,800) (PCGS VF35, $7,700) (PCGS XF40, $1,800-$9,800) (PCGS XF45, $8,900-$10,500) (PCGS AU50, $3900-$6,500) (PCGS AU53, $7,600-$9,400) (PCGS AU58, $13,800-$18,800) (NGC MS62, $15,300) (NGC MS65, $58,750)

1797 13 stars (NGC VG8, $2,800) (NGC F15, $4,900-$6,500) (PCGS VF25, $5,500-$9,000) (NGC VF35, $4900) (NGC XF40, $10,500) (NGC AU58, $40,500)

1797 15 stars (PCGS G4, $1,270) (NGC G6, $1,400) (PCGS VG10, $1,400-$2,250) (PCGS VF30, $1,700-$3,900) (PCGS F15, $2,350-$3,500) (PCGS VF20, $2,300-$2,800)

(PCGS VF30, 3,800) (NGC XF40, $2,300-$6,800) (NGC XF45, $7,200) (PCGS AU55, $6,200-$11,500) (NGC MS62, $24,200) (PCGS MS64, $47,000)

1797 16 stars (PCGS G4, $1,750) (ANACS VG8, $1270) (PCGS VG10, $2,500) (PCGS VF20, $1,500-$3,900) (PCGS VF25, $5,200) (PCGS XF45, $1,925-$7,500) (PCGS AU55, $4,300-$8,500) (ANACS AU58, $9,200) (PCGS MS66, $123,500)

1800 LIBEKTY – (PCGS G4, $1,400) (PCGS VG10, $1,500-$1,900) (NGC F15, $2,900) (PCGS VF35, $2,800-$7,400) (ANACS XF40, $1,400-$5,400) (PCGS AU58, $7,300-$17,250) (PCGS MS64, $31,000-$38,000) (PCGS MS65, $45,000-$80,500) (PCGS MS66, $111,700)

1811 1/2 (PCGS XF40, $4,025) 2017

1837 Large Date – (ANACS F15, $80) (NGG XF45, $345-$180) (NGC MS65, $1,400-$10,350) (NGC MS66, $1,900-$22,300) (NGC MS67, $5,800-$11,500) (NGC MS68, $43,700) (NGC PR66, $39,000)

1837 Small Date – (PCGS VG8, $60) (ANACS XF45, $175-$180) (NGC MS65, $1200-$10,500) (PCGS MS66, $2,900-$21,500) (PCGS MS67, $11,700-$23,000) (NGC PR67, $22,350)

1838-O no stars – (ANACS G4, $82-$150) (ANACS VG8, $184) (PCGS VF30, $240-$1,100) (ANACS XF45, $450-$4,900) (NGC AU58, $690-$4,700) (NGC MS62, $4,700-$10,950) (NGC MS64, $8,050-$25,300) (NGC MS65, $21,100- $28,750) (PCGS MS66, $18,400-$49,950)

1849 9/8 (ANACS AU50, $184) (PCGS MS67, $7000)

1849 9/6

1849 9 over widely placed 6

1853 over 53 no arrows (NGC MS66, $10,600-11,200) 2017

1853 over 53 (NGC MS66, $10,575-$11,200) 2017

1853 no arrows (PCGS AU58, $1,300-$8,225) (PCGS MS63, $1,500-$16,100) (NGC MS65, $1,600-$9,400) (PCGS MS66, $2,100-5,100) (NGC MS67, $6,000) (NGC MS68, $10,300-$12,925)

1853 arrows (ANACS G4, $17-$20) (ANACS VG8, $17-$50) (ANACS VF35, $53) (PCGS F12, $21-$55) (ANACS VF35, $25-$50) (ANACS XF45, $42-$90) (PCGS MS65, $795-$4,800) (NGC MS66, $1,600-13,225) (PCGS MS67, $4,800-$18,600)

1853-O arrows – (PCGS VG8, $30) (ANACS VF35, $42-$100) (PCGS XF45, $75-$2,000) (NGC MS65, $2,400-

$4,100) (PCGS MS66, $4,400-$5,400) (PCGS MS67, $15,200-$29,900)
1853-O no arrows – (ANACS XF45, $1,700-$2,000) (PCGS MS63, $14,500-$29,900) (PCGS MS64, $23,000) (PCGS MS65, $22,200-$37,600) 2017
1855/54 (PCGS MS62, $2,850)
1858 inverted date – (ANACS VG8, $37) (PCGS VF25, $155) (ANACS XF40, $140-$250) (PCGS MS64, $2,000) (NGC MS65, $1,750-$7,600) (PCGS MS66, $3200-$11,750)
1861 1/0 – (PCGS MS66, $2850) 2017

The poorly minted ½ dime is most likely subject to many flaws and perhaps some unknown errors. A collector should be aware of the numerous numbers of these coins with cleaning, plugs, and alterations. Many samples have bent or clips around the coin but they may be considered valuable because of the limited issues.

Chapter 9– Dimes
1796-1891 Early Dimes

The first dimes minted were in 1796. The first version, the draped bust dime was minted in 1796 and 1797.
The Heraldic eagle reverse was minted from 1796 through 1807. Capped bust dimes were minted from 1809 through 1837, followed by the liberty seated dimes dated from 1837 through 1891.

Variations and Errors
1797 13 stars - Very Fine $6000
1797 16 stars – Very Fine $5500
1798 8 over 7 13 stars – Very Fine $4500
1798 8 over 7 16 stars – Very Fine $1500
1811 11 over 9 – Very Fine $600
1823 3 over 2 small E's – Very Fine $165
1823 3 over 2 large E's – Very Fine $165
1828 large date – Very Fine $165
1828 small date – Very Fine $80
1830 large 10 cents – Very Fine $75
1803 small 10 cents – Very Fine $75
1838 small stars DDR (ANACS XF45, $220) 2015
1838 large stars DDR (ANACS XF40, $150) 2015
1838 partial drapery – Very Fine $50
1840 no drapery - Very Fine $90
1840 drapery - Very Fine $150
1853 no arrows – Very Fine - $350
1853 arrows – Very Fine - $25
1855 DDO (NGC MS63, $575) 2015
1856 small date – Very Fine $20
1856 large date – Very Fine $20
1871 DDO (ANACS PR63, $285) 2015
1873 close 3 – Very Fine $20
1873 open 3 – Very Fine $100
1876 DDO (PCGS VF30, $173) 2015
1876 DDR (PCGS MS62, $410) 2015
1876-CC DDO (NGC XF45, $160) 2015
1877-CC DDR (PCGS XF45 cleaned, $84) 2015
1889 DDR (PCGS VF30, $72) 2015

Dimes – Barber 1892 to 1916

With the production of the Barber dime, the mint was able to gain some perfection in the minting process. More attention to die use and maintaining the dies and hubs led to less error coins and variations.

This set is very accessible by collectors with the exception of a few coins with low mintages. The key coins to this set are the 1892-S, 1893-O, 1894-O, 1894-S (extremely rare), 1895, 1895-O, 1895-S, 1896-O, 1896-S, 1901-S, and the 1903-S. Note that the 1894-S has sold at auction for more than $1 million dollars in proof condition.

Variations and Errors

1893 3/2 – Very Fine $150
1893 S over S – (ANACS MS60, $155 - 200) 2017
1905-O micro O (NGC MS63, $4900) 2017

Dimes – Mercury 1916 to 1945

The most revered and widely collected US dime is the Mercury dime. Many Mercury dimes are available in all grades for the collector. There is no shortage of any date including the 1916-D Mercury dime. If the collector has the funds a 1916-D in most any condition can be procured readily from a coin dealer or at an on line auction site. A check of eBay shows that there is always a listing for a 1916-D Mercury dime on the site.

Above is a 1935 Mercury dime

Variations and Errors

1916-D D/D (ANACS XF40, $3,500) 2017
1928-S DDO (PCGS MS65, $1265) 2015
1929-S DDO (PCGS MS67, $950-$1,400)
1931-D DDO (ANACS AU55, $67) 2015

1931-D DDO/DDR (PCGS MS67 FB, $2,150) 2017
1931-S DDO (PCGS MS62, $115) (PCGS MS66 FB, $3,750) 2015
1936 DDO (PCGS MS62, $65) 2015
1937 DDO (ANACS MS64 FB, $40) 2015
1937-S DDO (NGC MS68, $472) 2015
1940-S DDO (ANACS MS65, $50) 2015
1942 over 1 (PCGS VF30, $176-$925) (PCGS XF45, $322-$1,250) (PCGS AU55, $825-$3,700) (PCGS AU58, $1,050-$2,100) (PCGS MS60, $2,100-$2,300) (PCGS MS62, $1,600-$3,700) (PCGS MS63, $2,300- $5,400) (PCGS MS63 FB, $5,500-$11,500) (PCGS MS64, $5,750-$13,500) (PCGS MS64 FB, $8,000-$9,775) (PCGS MS65, $9,775-$20,000) (PCGS MS65 FB, $15,000-$25,850) (PCGS MS66 FB, $13,500- $76,350)
1942-D 2/1 (NGC G6, $275) (PCGS VG10, $250-$350) (PCGS F12, $275-$475) (PCGS F15, $275-$400) (PCGS VF35, $375-$850) (PCGS XF45, $550-$1,250) (ANACS AU55, $975-$2,000) (NGC AU58, $900-$2,000) (PCGS MS60, $850-$4,300) (PCGS MS62, $3,700-$4,900) (PCGS MS63, $3,800-$7,400) (PCGS MS64, $3,800-$7,600) (NGC MS65, $6,900)
1942/1 D/D (NGC MS62, $3,000-$5,175) (ANACS AU55, $633) 2015
1943-S S/S Repunched mintmark (PCGS MS67, $2,800)
1945-S Micro S (PCGS MS63, $23) (PCGS MS64 NGC, $23) (PCGS MS65 FB, $500-$1,300) (ANACS MS65, $45) (PCGS MS66 FB, $675-$8,050) (PCGS MS67, $450-$7,600) (NGC MS68, $900) (PCGS MS68 FB, $14,950)

Dimes – Roosevelt 1946-

The Roosevelt dime mintage began in 1946 replacing the Mercury dime. Until 1965, all Roosevelt dimes were 90 percent silver and 10 percent copper. The vast majority of Roosevelt dimes minted before 1965 disappeared from circulation for the silver content. It is unknown how many silver coins were melted for the silver content.

Most silver Roosevelt dimes are in conditions above very good because of the removal from circulation when the price of silver escalated in the early 1970's. It is relatively easy to obtain a brilliant uncirculated collection of Roosevelt dimes at a reasonable cost.

The perfection of the Mint's processes has restricted the error coins to a few dates in the Roosevelt dime series.

Pictured above is a 2013-S Roosevelt dime

To date the Roosevelt dime is the only circulating coin to escape design modifications by the mint. Even when most of the U.S. coinage design changed in 1976 to display 1776-1976 as the date, the dime remained unchanged. The only change made to the coin was to add a P in 1980 to the obverse of the coin.

Variations and Errors

1941-D DDO (PCGS MS65 FB, $220) 2015

1946 D D/D (PCGS MS66, $50) 2016

1946 DDO (PCGS MS64, $30-$45) (PCGS MS65, $40-$135) 2014

1946 DDR (PCGS MS65, $40) 2016

1946 DDO and DDR (ANACS MS62, $35) (PCGS MS65, $40-$45) (PCGS MS67, $70-$75) 2016

1946-D DDR (ANACS MS63, $30-$35) 2017

1946-S DDO (PCGS MS66, $23) 2014

1946-S DDR (ANACS MS64, $35-$45) (ANACS MS65, $70) (PCGS MS66, $80-$140) (NGC MS67, $282) 2015/2017

1946-S/S DDR (ANACS AU53, $54-$104) (ANACS MS64, $30-$60) (PCGS MS65, $30-$55) (NGC MS66, $90-$95) (PCGS MS67, $540) 2015

1946-S Triple S DDR (NGC MS64, $30-$135) (NGC MS65, $40) 2016

1947-D DDO (PCGS MS65, $60) 2016

1947-S S/D (NGC MS64, $115) (PCGS MS66, $50-$165) 2016/2017

1947- S S/S (PCGS MS66, $50-$85) 2016

1947-S DDO (ANACS, MS65, $65) 2017

1947-S DDR (PCGS MS64, $100) (PCGS MS65, $95) (NGC MS67, $140-$375) 2015

1948 DDO (ANACS MS65, $235) 2017
1948-S S/S (PCGS MS66, $50) 2016
1949-S S/S (ANACS MS66, $30-$45) (NGC MS67, $50) 2017
1950 DDR (PCGS PR66, $300-$500) 2017
1950-D DDR die 1 (ANACS MS64, $23-$55) 2016
1950-S S/D (PCGS MS65, $85-$110) (PCGS MS66, $160-$300)
1950-S over inverted S (NGC MS65, $65-$85) (PCGS MS67, $625) 2017
1951 D/D (ANACS MS65, $49) (PCGS MS66, $210) 2017
1951-S S/S (PCGS MS66, $50) 2016
1952-D D/D (PCGS MS66, $175) 2017
1952-S S/S (PCGS MS66, $50) 2016
1953-D D over horizontal D (PCGS MS66, $50) 2016
1954 DDO (PCGS PR65, $55) (PCGS PR66, $45-$89) 2017
1954 DDR (PCGS MS65, $80) (PCGS MS66, $350-$400) (PCGS MS67, $100) 2016
1954-S S/S (PCGS MS65, $40) (PCGS MS66, $80- $90) 2016
1954-S No JS, designer initials (PCGS MS66, $165) 2017
1956 DDR (ANACS PR64, $60) 2017
1959-D Inverted D (PCGS MS65, $40-$90) (PCGS MS66, $100) 2016
1959-D D/D (PCGS MS64, $30-$35) (PCGS MS65, $50) (PCGS MS66, $110) 2016
1960 DDO (NGC PR64, $80-$90) (PCGS PR65 FB $155-$275) (PCGS PR65, $40-$80) (PCGS PR66, $70-$300) (PCGS PR67DCAM, $345-$529) (PCGS PR67, $105-$270) (PCGS PR68, $63-$995)
1960 DDR (ANACS MS64, $30) (NGC PR64, $30-$52) (ANACS PR65, $30) (NGC PR66, $60-$90) (PCGS PR68, $145-$375) 2015
1960- D/D (PCGS MS66, $130-$325) 2017
1961-D DDR (PCGS MS66, $50) 2016
1962-D D over horizontal D (PCGS MS66, $150) 2016
1963 DDO (ANACS PR64, $40) PCGS PR66, $90) (NGC PR67, $80-$85) (NGC PR69, $145) 2015
1963 DDR (PCGS PR64, $33-$150) (PCGS PR 65, $55-$200) (PCGS PR66, $30-$175) (PCGS PR67, $40-$375) (NGC PR68, $89-$710) (NGC PR69, $110-$150) 2017
1963 DDR (ANACS MS65, $21) (PCGS MS66, $155-$329) 2017
1963-D DDR (PCGS MS66, $90) 2017
1964 pointed 9 (PCGS MS66, $20) 2016

1964 pointed 9 (PCGS PR69, $110-$400) 2017
1964 blunt 9 (PCGS MS66, $20) 2016
1964 DDR (ANACS PR67, $30) 2017
1964-D stuck on one-cent planchet (PCGS MS64, $3,400-$4,300)
1964-D blunt 9 (PCGS MS66, $20) 2016
1964-D D/D (PCGS MS64, $35-$50) 2017
1964-D DDO (PCGS MS65, $800-$1,840) (PCGS MS66, $280) 2017
1964-D DDR (PCGS AU55, $55-$60) (NGC AU53, $150) (PCGS MS64, $165-$1,150) (PCGS MS65, $99-$2,500) 2015
1965 struck on silver planchet (ANACS AU55, $4,000-$8,625)
1968 DDO (ANACS PR64, $23) (PCGS MS65, $30) (PCGS MS67, $70-$75) 2016
1968-D struck on silver planchet (NGC AU55, $5,750)
1968 proof no S (PCGS PR66, $10,575-$18,400) (PCGS PR67, $11,500-$37,375) (PCGS PR68, $10-$48,875) (PCGS PR70, $5,000)
1968-S DDO (NGC PR67 $50-$110) (NGC PR68, $185) 2015
1968-S DDR (ANACS PR64, $27) (ANACS PR65, $25) (NGC PR67, $125) 2015
1968-S S/S (PCGS PR66, $425) 2017
1969 reverse of 1968 (PCGS MS65, $50) 2016
1969-D/D (NGC MS64, $30) (PCGS MS65, $30) 2014
1970 reverse of 1968 (PCGS MS66, $50) 2016
1970 proof no S (NGC PR66, $440) (PCGS PR67, $285-$750) (PR68, $600-$6,037) (PCGS PR69, $5,750-$6,000)
1970-D triple struck – saddle type (PCGS MS66, $1,900)
1970-D DDR (PCGS MS64, $79) (ANACS MS65, $50-$60) (PCGS MS66, $60-$100) 2015/2017
1970-D reverse of 1968 (PCGS MS66, $50-$85) 2016
1970 proof no S (PCGS PR66, $565) (NGC, PR67, $515-$1,100) (PCGS PR68, $1,300) (PCGS PR69, $1,600-$5,100) 2017
1975-S S/S (PCGS PR69, $885) 2017
1977 die cap obverse (NGC MS69, $1,725)
1979-S Type 1 (PCGS PR70, $85-$300) 2017
1979-S Type 2 (PCGS PR70, $85-$425) 2017
1981-S Type 1 (PCGS PR70, $100-$1,350) 2017
1981-S Type 2 (PCGS PR70, $105-$510) 2017

1982 no P (NGC AU58, $75) (PCGS MS64, $95-$140) (PCGS MS65, $110-$375) (PCGS MS66, $240-$440) (PCGS MS67, $290-$800) (PCGS MS68, $995-$2,185)
1983 proof no S (PCGS PR66, $950) (PCGS PR67, $450-$1,000) (PCGS PR68, $450-$1,955) (PCGS PR69, $1000-$1,955) (PCGS PR70, $18-$8,225)
1998 struck on one-cent (PCGS MS64, $1,850-$4,450)
1999 stuck multiple times – uncertified $2,300
1999 Triple bonded multiple struck (NGC MS64, $3,000) 2016
2007-D triple struck on aluminum feeder finger (PCGS MS64, $3,300)

Chapter 10 – Twenty Cent 1875-1878

Perhaps a mint experiment that that never gained popularity; was the twenty cent piece which only lasted four years. The mint produced two years for circulation, the 1875 and the 1876. The 1877 and 1878 mintages were available in proof only. The 1876CC coin is very rare and can bring a value of several hundred thousand at auction.

Above is an 1876 Twenty-Cent piece

The 1877 and 1878 mintages are 510 and 600 pieces respectively. These are so rare that it has been difficult to locate any that have recently sold at auction.

Variations and Errors
1875-S Doubled "$" mintmark (NGC MS65, $3220) 2015

Chapter 11– Quarters 1796-date

1796-1807 Draped Bust

Above is an 1807 Draped Bust Quarter

Draped Bust Quarter Errors
1806 6/5 (PCGS MS64, $65,000)

1815-1838 Liberty Cap
There were no quarters minted from 1808 through 1814. The mint changed the design of the quarter in 1815 from the flowing hair design to the liberty cap design.

Pictured above is an 1815Liberty cap quarter

Variations and Errors
1818 8/5 (ANACS G4, $65-100) (NGC G6, $160-$230) (PCGS VF30, $625-$1,300) (PCGS XF45, $600-$2,000) (PCGS AU55, $1,000-$2,900) (PCGS MS64, $4,000-$22,000) (PCGS MS65 $7,500-$56,000) (PCGS MS66, $14,950) (NGC MS67, $176,250-$182,125)
1819 Large 9 (NGC XF45, $1,800-$2,700) (NGC AU58, $2,300-$7650) (NGC MS63, $5,400-$7,000) (NGC MS64, $16,500-$30,600) (PCGS MS65, $28,000)

1819 Small 9 (ANACS G4, $55-$350) (NGC VG8, $100-$1,000) (NGC F12, $110-$1,000) (NGC VF35, $745-$1,200) (NGC XF45, $1,200-$3,200) (PCGS AU58, $1,600-$8,800) (PCGS MS63, $4,300-$8,600) (NGC MS64, $15,275-$23,500)

1820 Small O (PCGS VG8, $90-$110) (NGC VF25, $400-$4,800) (NGC XF45, $775-$1,200) (NGC AU55, $1,800-$4,900) (MS64, $11,100-$16,000) (NGC MS66, $41,000) (PCGS MS67, $63,250)

1820 Medium O (PCGS MS63, $5,100) (PCGS MS66, $37,600-$76,300)

1820 Large O (ANACS G6, $50-$125) (PCGS VG10, $100-$250) (PCGS F12, $200-$375) (NGC VF35, $250-$1,100) (NGC XF45, $975-$3,200) (PCGS AU55, $2,500-$6,400) (NGC MS64, $3,900 -$13,250) (PCGS MS65, $24,000-$54,000) (PCGS MS66, $38,000-$64,500)

1822 $.25/$.50 (NGC AG3, $3,500-$6,900) (PCGS G6, $1,000-$6,900) (PCGS VG10, $265-$16,100) (NGC F15, $19,100) (PCGS VF35, $8,600) (PCGS AU58, $8,400) (NGC MS63, $69,000) (NGC MS66, $180,000-$195,500)

1823 3/2 (PCGS G4, $37,500-$43,100) (PCGS VG10, $40,000) (NGC VF30, $57,500-$74,500)

1824 4/2 (PCGS AG3, $200-$450) (PCGS G6, $550-$1,200) (PCGS VG10, $250-$1,500) (PCGS F15, $1,500-$2,000) (PCGS VF35, $2,200-$3,700) (ANACS XF45, $2,800-$6,900) (NGC AU58, $7,000-$16,400) (PCGS MS64, $115,000) (PCGS MS66, $28,200-$32,900) (PCGS PR64, $396,500)

1827 proof using a 1823 die (NGC AU58, $8,200) (PCGS PR63, $32,000-$185,000) (PCGS PR64, $46,000-$411,000) (NGC PR66, $63,000-$86,000)

1828 $.25/ $50 (NGC VG10, $1,600-$13,800) (NGC F15, $3,000-$19,300) (NGC VF35, $2,500-$20,000) (PCGS XF45, $5,800-$7,300) (NGC MS65, $108,000-$123,200) (NGC MS66, $184,000) (NGC MS67, $282,000-$352,000) (PCGS PR63, $189,000) (PCGS PR65, $62,000-$229,000)

1831 Small letters
1831 Large letters

1838-1865 Seated liberty
The seated liberty type quarter replaced the liberty cap design in 1838 with both types minted in 1838.

Pictured above is an 1847 Seated Liberty Quarter

Variations and Errors
1841-O DDO (ANACS AU58 Details, $235) 2015
1842 small date – Proof Only $35,000
1842 large date – Very Fine $200
1842-O small date – Very Fine $1,500
1842-O large date - Very Fine $35
1844 DDO (ANACS AU50, $525) 2015
1847 DDO (ANACS VF20, $30) 2015
1847 DDR (ANACS XF40, $110) 2015
1853 no arrows or rays
1853 3/4

1866-1891 Seated liberty Motto Above Eagle
The mint changed the seated liberty coin in 1866 by adding a motto above the eagle "In God We Trust." In 1873 some mintages contained arrows at the date. The 1874 issues all contained arrows at the date. From 1875 forward no arrows appeared at the date.

Varieties and Errors
1873 no arrows
1873-CC no arrows
1873 with arrows at the date
1873-CC with arrows at the date
1877 S/S (NGC MS62,$1000) 2017

1892-1916 Barber Quarter

This series of quarters is very affordable for most dates in all grades from good through extra fine enabling a collector to locate most dates.

The rarest coins in this set are the 1896-S and the 1901-S mintages. The 1901-S escalates in value from $4,000 in good to over $10,000 in extra fine. At auction one 1901-S Barber quarter in about good condition sold for close to $3,000.

Most Barber quarters in grades of MS65 or higher can bring over $2500 at auction.

Variations and Errors
1892 DDR (ANACS MS62, $255) 2015
1892-O DDO (NGC AU58, $285) 2015

1916-1930 Standing Liberty Quarter

Above is a 1926 standing liberty quarter

The mint overlapped production of the standing liberty quarter with the last year of mintage for the Barber quarter. This made the 1916 standing liberty quarter as the most valuable coin in the collection with values starting at $1,500 in good and over $5,000 in extra fine.

Two variations of the 1916 coin were part of the mintage in Philadelphia, San Francisco, and Denver with coins minted with no stars and with stars under the eagle. The version with stars continued from 1917 through the end of the collection in 1930.

Pictured above is a 1918/7 standing liberty quarter

Variations and Errors
1918 8/7 (PCGS MS64, $25,150-$149,500) (PCGS MS65, $46,000-$109,500) (NGC MS66, $97,750)
1928-S over S (NGC MS65 Full Head, $690) 2017

1932- Date Washington Quarters
The transformation of all mint issues with former Presidents on the major circulating coins continued with placing George Washington on the quarter replacing the liberty quarter.

There are many DDO Washington quarter errors with a wide range of values based upon the mintage, demand, and the condition.

Above is a 1934 double die

Above is a 1937 doubled die obverse with a doubling of the words "IN GOD WE TRUST." The defined doubling is not as robust in this design as in some other mint doubling errors but it is an authentic DDO coin.

Washington Quarter Errors

Above is a 1974-D Washington quarter

Variations and Errors
1932 DDO (ANACS MS62, $125-$235) 2014
1934 DDO (ANACS VG10, $46) (ANACS AU50, $175-$315) (PCGS MS63, $3,737-$4,300) (PCGS MS64, $3,200-$3,500) (PCGS MS65, $3,700-$6,600) (PCGS MS66, $4,887- $9,500)
1934 DDO die 1 (ANACS F12, $33) 2015
1934 DDR (ANACS VG10, $46)
1936 DDO (NGC G, $16) (ANACS AU58, $100)
1937 DDO (ANACS, F12, $322) (ANACS MS63, $3,725-$6,325) (PCGS MS64, $4,300- $14,950) (PCGS MS66, $19,550)
1937-D DDO (ANACS MS65, $98-$115) 2015
1937-S DDO (ANACS MS64, $271) (PCGS MS67, $2420) 2014
1938 DDO (PCGS AU58, $175) 2015

1939 DDO die 1 (ANACS MS63, $92) 2015
1939 DDO die 3 (ANACS MS64, $46) 2014
1939-D DDO (ANACS MS64, $37) 2015
1939-S DDO (ANACS MS63, $92) (ANACS MS64, $196)
(PCGS MS66, $415) 2014
1940-D DDO (ANACS MS63, $145)
1940 D/D (ANACS MS63, $155) 2016
1940-S DDO (ANACS MS64, $42-$60) 2014
1940-S DDO and DDR (ANACS MS64, $42) 2014
1940-S/S DDO (ANACS MS63, $92) 2015
1941 DDO (NGC/PCGS MS66, $75-$207)
1941 DDR (ANACS AU55, $20) (ANACS MS63, $50) 2014
1941-D DDR (PCGS MS65, $223) 2014
1942 DDO (ANACS MS64, $25) 2016
1942 DDR (ANACS MS62, $35-$50) 2015
1942-D DDO (ANACS F12, $100) (ANACS VF35, $175-
$345) (ANACS AU50, $750-$1,600) (PCGS MS63, $3,450)
(PCGS MS64, $5,175) (PCGS MS66, $4,300)
1943 DDO (ANACS MS63, $45-$100) (ANACS MS65, $275)
1943-D DDO (ANACS XF45, $21) (ANACS MS64, $173)
2014
1943-S DDO (ANACS AU55, $400) (PCGS MS64, $1,550)
(PCGS MS65, $3,400-$9,500) (PCGS MS66, $6,325-
$9,500)
1944 DDO (ANACS MS64, $70) 2015
1944-D DDO (PCGS MS63, $31-$55) 2014
1944-S DDO (ANACS MS63, $25) (PCGS MS67, $700)
1945 DDO die 1 (ANACS XF45, $24-$50) 2015
1945 DDO die 2 (NGC MS66, $95-$207)
1945 DDO die 5 (ANACS MS64, $21) 2015
1945-D DDO (ANACS MS63, $70-$100) 2015
1946-D D/S (ANACS MS64, $46)
1947-S/S (ANACS MS64, $50-$100) 2015
1949-D DDO (ANACS MS64, $30-$100) 2015
1950 DDR (ANACS MS65, $21-$30) (PCGS MS66, $115)
1950-D DDR (NGC MS63, $58) 2015
1950-D D/D (ANACS MS63, $62) 2015
1950-D D/S (ANACS VG10, $23) (PCGS F12, $47) (NGC
VF30, $48) (PCGS EF45, $126-$138) (ANACS MS63, $62)
(NGC MS64, $2,358) (PCGS MS65, $4,025-$7,500) (PCGS
MS66, $3,737-$23,000) (NGC MS67, $4,000)
1950-S S/D (ANACS F15, $39) (PCGS VF30, $72-$115)
(ANACS EF45, $144) (NGC/PCGS MS65, $550-$2,875)
(PCGS MS66, $495-$4,255)

(NGC MS67, $3,600-$3,737)
1950-S S/S (ANACS MS65, $161)
1952 Reverse Brockage (NGC MS64, $4700) 2016
1952-D Huge D (ANACS VF25, $50) 2017
1953 DDO (PCGS PR65, $255) 2015
1953-D DDR (ANACS MS63, $30) 2015
1954 DDR (ANACS PR65, $30-$85) 2015
1956 DDR (ANACS MS65, $25-$50) 2015
1957 DDR (ANACS MS64, $18) 2015
1959 DDO (PCGS PR66, $60-$150) 2015
1959-D DDR (ANACS MS64, $14-$50) 2015
1960 DDR (PCGS PR65, $81) (PCGS PR66, $121)
1961 DDO (PCGS PR66, $70) 2015
1962 DDO die 1 (ANACS PR67, $23-$50) 2015
1962 DDO die 4 (ANACS MS65, $70) 2015
1962-D struck on quarter planchet (NGC MS62, $2,000) 2016
1963 DDO (ANACS MS64, $30-$80) (PCGS MS66, $305)
1963 DDR (NGC MS64, $40-$80) (ANACS MS65, $50)
1964 DDO (PCGS MS63, $23-$55) 2014
1964-D DDR (PCGS MS62, $95) 2015
1964-D DDO (PCGS MS62, $25-$50) 2015
1965 struck on silver planchet (PCGS AU58, $14,500) 2016
1965 DDO (PCGS AU55, $575) 2014
1966 DDR (PCGS XF45, $925) 2015
1967 DDO SMS (NGC MS67, $150-$230)
1967 DDR (ANACS MS66, $20-$50) 2015
1968-D DDR (PCGS MS64, $375) 2014
1968-S DDO (PCGS PR66, $374) 2014
1968-S DDR (PCGS PR66, $196) 2015
1969-D D/D (PCGS MS65, $25-$50) 2016
1969-S DDO (PCGS PR65, $300) 2015
1970-D DDO (PCGS MS65, $250-$300) 2014
1970-D DDR (PCGS MS65, $242) 2015
1971 DDR (PCGS AU58, $1,380) 2014
1971-D DDR (PCGS XF40, $1,100) 2015
1972 DDO (ANACS, MS60, $31)
1973 struck on cent planchet (NGC MS65, $1,400) 2016
1976-D DDO (PCGS AU58, $690) 2014
1990-S DDO (PCGS MS66, $350) 2016

State Quarter

1999-P CT – triple struck (ANACS MS63, $605) 2014

1999-P PA – struck on experimental planchet – (PCGS MS66, $6,325) 2014

1999-P 170-degree rotation (PCGS MS62, $300) 2014

1999-D 135-degree rotation (PCGS MS65, $200) 2017

1999-D DE – clad layer missing (PCGS MS63, $350) 2014

1999-D DE struck on nickel planchet (PCGS MS64, $412) 2016

1999-S District of Columbia DDO (PCGS MS66, $3,000) 2017

2000-P MA – clad layer missing (PCGS MS64, $368) 2014

2000-P MD – struck on 5C (NGC MS67, $1,495) 2014

2001-P NY – double struck (PCGS MS66, $432) 2014

2001-D VT – clad layer missing (PCGS MS64, $238)

2000-P IN – struck on a dime planchet (PCGS MS64, $4,000) 2017

2002-P LA – filled dies (NGC MS67, $33) 2017

2002-D TN – struck on a dime planchet (NGC MS65, $4830) 2017

2004-D IA – clad layer missing (PCGS MS63, $520) 2014

2004-P FL – struck on 5C (PCGS MS67, $1600) 2014

2004-D WI – extra leaf high (PCGS MS63, $50-$175) (PCGS MS64, $55-$135) (PCGS MS65, $65-450) (PCGS MS66, $90-$2,500) (NGC MS67, $500-$2,700) 2014[26]

2004-D WI – extra leaf low (PCGS MS63, $50-$175) MS64, $55-$135) (PCGS MS65, $65-450) (PCGS MS66, $90-$920) (NGC MS67, $500-$1,150) 2014

2005-P MN – Extra tree (PCGS MS65, $25-$89) 2014

2005-D MN – Extra-tree (PCGS MS68, $85) 2017

2005-P MN – DDO (PCGS MS65, $150) 2014

2005-P MN – DDR (PCGS MS65, $150) 2014

2005-D MN – DDO (PCGS MS68, $90) 2016

America the Beautiful

2015 Homestead DDR – double pump in window (NGC MS65, $50) 2017

---

[26] The auction results provided a very large range of prices paid for these coins in grades shown. There is some over-lap from grade to grade. Auction results in the last couple of years' reveals falling prices for these coins.

Double pump in the window

Chapter 12– Half Dollars 1794-date

The first half dollar issued by the mint went into circulation in 1794. Many mint designs and variations have followed since the first half dollar mintage.

Flowing Hair
The flowing hair design of 1794 and 1795 are rare coins since the mintage of the 1794 was 5,300 and the mintage for the 1795 was around 13,000.
In 1795, the mint issued three variations of the coin.
1795 Two Leaf Design
1795 Three Leaf Design
1795 Re-Cut Date

Pictured above is a 1975 flowing hair design

1796-97 Small Eagle Half
Variations and Errors
1796 15 stars
1796 16 stars

1801-07 Draped Bust Half
Variations and Errors
1803 Small Three
1803 Large Three
1805 five over four
1806 six over five
1806 inverted six
1806 knobbed six
1806 knobbed six with large stars

1806 knobbed six stem not through the claw of the eagle

1807-36 Turban Head
Variations and Errors
1807 small stars
1807 large stars
1807 .50 over .25
1808 8 over 7
1812 12 over 11
1813 .50C over UNI (NGC, VF35 4.3K)
1814 14 over 13
1815 15 over 12
1817 17 over 13.
1817 over 4
1818 over 7
1819 over 18 with a large 9
1820 over 19
1822 over 21
1823 type 1 three
1823 type 2 three
1824 over 21 with other over dates
1827 over 6 and a curled 2
1829 over 27
1830 small zero
1830 large zero
1832 small letters
1832 large letters
1836 lettered edge with 50 over 00

1836-39 Turban Head / Capped Bust / Reed Edge
No significant variations during this mintage found by the writer.

Pictured above is an 1839 Turban head half-dollar

80

1839- 1866 Liberty Seated Variations and Errors
1839 Drapery
1839 No Drapery
1840 small letters
1840 large letters
1840-O small O
1840-O large O
1844 doubled die
1846 7 over 6
1853 with arrows
1853 no arrows

Pictured above is an 1870 seated half

1866- 1891 Liberty Seated Variations and Errors
1873-CC no arrows
1873-CC arrows
1873-S no arrows
1873-S arrows
1873 no arrows
1873 arrows

Pictured above – 1866-S seated half dollar
1892- 1915 Barber half

The Barber half mintage is relatively free of pronounced error coins as recorded in major coin guides or on online sites.

Pictured above is a 1906 barber half

1892-O Micro-O (PCGS G6 $3,525 – $4,993) (PCGS VG8, $6,450 – $7,475) (PCGS F12, $3,105) (PCGS VF30, $12,350) (PCGS MS65, $34,500 - $92,000) 2017
1893 DDR (ANACS Cleaned MS60, $630) 2017

1916-1947 Walking Liberty
In 1916, the mint-mark appeared on the obverse of the coin. The mint-mark on the coin appeared on either the front or the reverse of the coins in 1917. Both D and S mint-marks appear on 1917 coins on either the obverse or the reverse of the coin. These are very strong-dated and mint marked coins, which provide collectors with ample stock from the lowest grades through extra fine condition.
The mint did not make half dollars in this series in 1922 and from 1924 through 1926 and again from 1930 through 1932. Only San Francisco minted Walking Liberty halves in 1923, 1927, 1928, and 1933. The most common dates are in the 1940's and collectors should have no problem locating these dates in circulated condition.

Pictured above is a 1917 walking liberty half

Variations and Errors
1916-D D/D (ANACS MS62, $290) 2017

82

1921 double struck (ANACS MS61, $16,100)
1936 DDO (PCGS MS65, $320 - $350) 2016
1936-D DDO (PCGS MS65, $375 - $690) (PCGS MS66, $750) 2016
1939-S DDO (PCGS MS67, $1,120 - $1,750) 2016
1942 DDO (ANACS AU55, $35) 2016
1941-S S/S (ANACS AU55, $35) (PCGS MS64, $255) (PCGS MS65, $700 - $1,290) (PCGS MS66, $305) 2016
1942 DDR (PCGS MS65, $430 - $2,585) (PCGS MS66, $940) 2017
1942 struck on a silver quarter planchet (PCGS MS65, $17,600) 2016
1942-D DDO (ANACS MS65, $140) 2016
1943-D 3/2 (PCGS VG10. $13) 2017
1945 DDR (ANACS MS64, $95) 2016
1945 struck on dime planchet (NGC MS64, $42,000) 2016
1946 DDR (ANACS F15, $16) (NGC VF30, $65) (NGC XF45, $70 - $120) (PCGS MS66, $6,100 -$7,000) 2016
1946-S DDR (ANACS MS65, $225) 2016
1946-S S/S (NGC MS66, $215) 2017

1948-63 Ben Franklin
There are a few major error coins in the series that are widely noted. Some off mintages of a 1955 and 1956 coin appeared and collectors deemed it as the "bugs bunny" coin but most major coin guides do not list this coin as an error. Although there is not a lot of recognition, coin collectors do pay a premium for the Bugs Bunny half.

Pictured above is a 1950 Franklin half

Variations and Errors
1948 Obverse Die Clash (PCGS MS63 FBL, $89) 2017

83

1948 DDR (NGC MS64 FBL, $84) (PCGS MS65, $84 - $647) (NGC MS66 FBL, $525) 2017
1948-D DDR (PCGS MS66, $1,035)
1950 DDO (PCGS PR66, $390) 2015
1952 struck on quarter planchet (NGC AU58, $1,400) 2016

Above is a 1952 Half struck on a quarter planchet.

Variations and Errors
1955 struck on 5 cent planchet (NGC MS63, $3,650) 2016
1956 DDO (ANACS MS64, $43) (PCGS PR65, $153) (PCGS PR68, $575)
1955 Bugs Bunny (PCGS MS65, $200)
1956 Bug Bunny (PCGS MS66, $240)
1956 struck on quarter planchet (PCGS MS65, $1,650) 2016
1956 DDO (PR67 Cameo, $280) 2016
1956 DDR (PCGS PR68, $2,990)
1959 DDR (NGC MS65, $80) 2016
1960 DDO (NGC PR66, $173) (PCGS PR67, $382)
1961 DDR (PCGS PR66, $36-$190)
1962 Struck on a quarter planchet (NGC MS63, $2,000) 2015
1963-D struck on quarter planchet (NGC MS65, $5,000) 2016

Kennedy Half 1964-
The Kennedy half- dollar was never common in circulation. Some experts have interpreted the lack of usage as inability to use the coin in vending machines, or being too heavy to carry in pockets, and that the early mintages with hoarded by people for nostalgic reasons.
Casinos used most of the Kennedy half mintage for the slot machines before the use of paper payout forms. Millions of

Kennedy halves wore beyond recognition from use in slot machines.

Kennedy half mintages:

The 1964 issues are silver and command this premium
Mintages from 1965 through 1969 contain 40 percent silver.
The 1970 issue coin comes in proof only.
Kennedy halves minted for circulation from 1971 through 1986.
In 1987, Kennedy halves appeared in proof sets only.
The mint resumed circulation issues in 1988 and stopped minting for circulation in 2000.
In 2001 through 2004, the mint made all issues of the Kennedy half for mint and proof sets.
The 2005 mintage is in circulation.
From 2006 to date all Kennedy half production continued for proof sets. The mint has been offering rolls of Kennedy halves for sale on their web site for a number of years. It is possible that some of these rolled coins will reach circulation in the future.

Kennedy half-dated 1964

Variations and Errors
1964 accented hair (PCGS PR64, $50) 2017
1964 DDO (ANACS PR66, $10)
1964-D DDO (ANACS MS64, $21) 2016
1964-D D/D (PCGS MS 65, $100) 2017
1964-D Struck on a quarter planchet (NGC $1,750) 2016
1964-D Struck on nickel planchet (PCGS MS64, $3,525) 2016
1965 DDR (PCGS MS65, $600) 2016
1966 DDO SMS (PCGS SP65, $20-$28) (PCGS SP66, $47-$89) (PCGS SP67, $56-$126) (PCGS MS67, $161)
1966 Doubled profile (NGC MS67, $48)
1966 DDO/DDR (ANACS MS66, $25)
1966 no "FG" (PCGS SMS MS64, $60) 2015

85

1966 struck on quarter planchet (NGC MS63, $882) 2016
1967 DDR (ANACS MS66, $27)
1968-S DDO (ANACS PR63, $10)
1968-S DDR (ANACS PR66, $9) (H, ANACS PR67, $16)
1969-S DDO/DDR (ANACS PR67, $16)
1971 DDO (PCGS MS65, $100)
1971-D DDO (PCGS MS63, $24)
1971-S DDO (PCGS PR66, $50)
1973-D DDO (PCGS MS65, $200)
1974-D DDO (ANACS AU55, $45) 2016
1776-1976 DDR (PCGS MS65, $500) 2016
1977-D Struck on 40% silver planchet (NGC AU55, $4,200)
1977-D DDO (PCGS MS65, $650)
1982-P no "FG" (PCGS MS63, $50) 2014

Chapter 13 – Dollars 1794-date

1794-95 Flowing Hair Design
The silver dollar mintage began in 1794 and much like the half dollar the first design last only two years. The rarity of the 1794 silver dollar could bring over $20,000 in circulated condition.

1795-1804 Draped Bust
The mint changed the design in 1795 and minted both versions of the flowing hair and the draped bust types.

Variations and Errors
1797 small letters
1797 large letters
1797 9 stars to the left
1797 7 stars to the right
1797 10 stars left and 6 right

1836-1839 Liberty Seated
Silver dollars minted during this time contained an eagle on the reverse of the coin. All three mintages of this coin are extremely valuable.

1840-1866 Liberty Seated No Motto
There are no well-known error coins during this span of silver dollars. The 1866 mintage was struck in proof only and there are very few known.

1866-1873 Liberty Seated with motto
In 1866, the motto "In God We Trust" became part of the silver dollar design. There was a mintage of the 1873 coin at the San Francisco mint; however, no one has yet to reveal a coin in a collection. No one knows what happened to the 1873-S coins and if someone were to locate this coin, it would bring millions.

Variations and Errors
1841-O DDO (ANACS AU58 details, $235) 2015
1844 DDO (ANACS AU50, $525) 2015
1847 DDO (ANACS VF20, $30) 2015
1847 DDR (ANACS XF40, $110) 2015
1876 DDR (ANACS AU details, $345) 2015
1877-S DDR (PCGS XF45, $259) 2015

1873-1885 Trade Dollars

The mint needed to produce a dollar coin that competed with the European coins of the same denomination. Since the European coins were larger, the US had issues trading with the silver dollar. The mint produced the trade dollar with more silver content. The coin is thicker than other silver dollars of that time. Shortly after the mintage of this coin, the US Treasury department made the coin illegal to use in domestic trade, restricting the coins for use in international transactions.

Pictured above is a typical US trade dollar

1878-1904 1921 Morgan Dollar

Pictured above is an 1886 Morgan Dollar

The mint returned to the regular production of the silver dollar for domestic use in 1878 changing the design known as the Morgan dollar. The Morgan dollar is most widely collected because of the numbers of coins available to collectors at a reasonable cost. Leroy C. Van Allen and A. George Mallis cataloged most of the Morgan dollar variations and errors. Together the two collectors designated the error classifications as VAM's. Thousands of cataloged VAM coins are available to the collector at reasonable prices. The VAM designation will always be a part of the encapsulation services such as NGC and PCGS. It is within the scope of this book to provide realized auction sales of some VAM coins so that the collector has a reference value

Variations and Errors
1878 8 Tail Feathers – proof like (NGC MS61, $420) 2015
1878 8 Tail Feathers (PCGS MS62, $207)
1878 7 Tail Feathers reverse of 1878 VAM 121, VAM 31 (PCGS MS62, $195.50)
1878 7 Tail Feathers Tripled Eye VAM 166 (PCGS AU50, $2,000) 2015
1878 Rev of 1879 (ANACS AU50, $40) 2015
1878 Triple Blossoms VAM 44 (PCGS MS61, $14,000)
1878 Triple Eyelid VAM 50 (NGC AU58, $176)
1878 Spiked Eye (PCGS Unc Details, $350)
1878 DDO 8TF (NGC MS62, $282) 2015
1878-CC Doubled Leaves (NGC AU5, $915) 2015
1878-S Doubled "RIB" (NGC MS63, $104) 2015
1879-O O/O (ANACS MS60, $260) 2017
1880 80/79 VAM 8 Ears (PCGS MS66, $517)
1880-O 80/79 (PCGS MS62, $435) (PCGS MS63, $488)
1880-O Hang Nail (ANACS AU58, $65)
1880-O DDO (PCGS VF20, $149)
1881 DDO (NGC MS64, $825) 2015
1881-O Double Ear VAM 27 (PCGS, AU53, $140)
1882-O O/O (PCGS MS63, $100) 2015
1882-O O/S (PCGS AU55, $235)
1882-O O/S Flush S VAM 3 (PCGS AU55, $235)
1883 Sextupled Stars VAM 10 (NGC XF45, $300)
1883-O O/O VAM 4 (PCGS MS63, $80)
1883-O Partial E Reverse (PCGS MS63, $75)
1884 Partial E Reverse (NGC MS62, $100)
1884 Large Dot VAM 3 (PCGS AU55, $75)
1884-O Misplaced 88 VAM 25 (NGC MS63, $85)
1884-O O over O Doubled Ear VAM 10 (NGC MS65, $138) 2015
1884-O DDO Eyelid (NGC MS64, $106)
1884-O/O (PCGS MS64, $126.50)
1886 Line in 6 VAM 1A (ANACS MS65, $130)
1886 DDR Arrows (NGC MS65, $141) 2015
1886 DDR (ANACS MS62, $57) 2015
1886 Doubled Arrows VAM 17 (ANACS MS64)
1886-O Rotated Dies (NCG AU50, $200)
1886-O Clashed E VAM 1A (NGC AU55, $200)
1886-O O/O VAM 7 (NGC AU55, $440)
1887 DDO VAM 5 (NGC MS64, $115) 2015
1887 Donkey Tail VAM 25A (NGC VF details, $65)
1887 Gator Eye DDO (NGC MS65, $177) 2015
1887 7/6 VAM 2 (NGC AU58, $165)

1887-O Clash VAM 30A (NGC AU53, $95)
1887-O Doubled 1 VAM 2 (NGC MS61, $99) 2015
1887-O Doubled Stars VAM 5 (NGC MS62, $200)
1887-O DDO VAM 22A (NGC AU53, $115)
1887-S S/S (PCGS XF45, 99) (PCGS MS63, $253)
1888 DDO Doubled Ear VAM 11 (NGC MS63, $66) 2015
1888 DDR VAM 12A (NGC MS63, $94) 2015
1888 Doubled Ear VAM 11A (NGC MS63, $80)
1888-O Clashed E VAM 1A (ANACS (NGC MS62, $175)
1888-O O/O DDR (NGC XF45, $374) 2015
1888-O Oval VAM 4 (PCGS XF40, $65)
1888-O Oval VAM 6 (PCGS XF40, MS60, $132) $60)
1888-O Oval VAM 17 (PCGS XF45, $75-$85) (NGC MS60, $212) 2017
1888-O Oval VAM 21 (NGC AU55, $110)
1888-O DDO (ANCS XF40, $165) (NGC XF45, $360-$700)
1888-O DDO (ANACS MS60, $12,925) 2017
1888-O DDO Deep Mirror Proof like (PCGS MS60, $25,300 2017
1888-O DDR Arrows (NGC MS65, $500) 2015
1888-O Hot Lips VAM 4 (NGC F15, $85)
1888-O Hot Lips DDO VAM 4 (NGC XF45, $260) (PCGS MS60, 5,175) 2017
1888-O Doubled Arrows VAM 9 (NGC MS63, $70)
1888-O Scarface VAM-1B4 (PCGS MS60, $2,100-$3,200) 2017
1889 VAM 1 (ANACS AU58, $13) 2017
1889 VAM 28A (ANACS MS60, $51) 2017
1889 Bar Wing VAM 19A (NGC MS61, $85) (PCGS MS66, $2,350)
1889 Doubled Ear (ANACS MS60, $62) (NGC MS65, $329) 2015
1889 DDO Doubled Ear VAM18 (NGC MS60, $53) 2017

1889 Doubled Ear VAM16 (PCGS MS66, $825) 2017
1889-O Clashed E VAM 1A (NGC VF30, $200)
1889-O Micro O (PCGS VF30, $50) 2015
1890-CC Tail Bar (NGC G4, $94-$115) (NGC VG10, $124 -159) (NGC VF35, $258-$345) (PCGS XF45, $176 – 423) (PCGS MS63, $1,950 - $3,220) (NGS MS64, $2,530 - $10,575) (NGC MS65, $9,200 - $28,850) 2017
1891-CC Spitting Eagle VAM3 – (NGC G6, $72) (NGC VG10, $94) **(**NGC VF25, $115) (NGC VF25, $117 - $119) (PCGS XF45, $130-188) (NGC MS60, $184 - $2,000) (PCGS MS65, $2.703 - $6,465) (PCGS MS66, $13,800) 2017
1890-O Doubled Ear and Leaves VAM 20NGC (NGC VF30, $200)

1890-O Weak Comet VAM 10A (NGC MS62, $115)
1891-O Weak Clashed E, VAM 3A (NGC XF45, $300)
1892-O DDO (PCGS XF40, $38) 2015
1895 S over Horizontal S (NGC MS60, $1,825) 2017
1896 DDO (NGC MS64, $135) 2015
1896 Misplaced Date VAM 19 (ANACS MS63, $60)
1896 8 In Denticle (PCGS MS63, $80)
1896-O Shifted Date VAM 19 (NGC AU details, $65)
1897 Doubled Stars VAM 8 (NGC MS62, $90)
1897-O Micro O VAM 6 (ANACS VF30, $28) 2917
1900 DDR (NGC MS64, $112) 2015
1900 Doubled Arrows (NGC MS63, $84) 2015
1900 Misplaced Date, Double Olives VAM 16 (NCG MS63, $110)
1900-O O/CC (PCGS MS64, $865) (PCGS MS65, $1,670 - $2,600)
1900-O Doubled Stars (PCGS MS65, $173) 2015
1901 DDR Shifted Eagle (PCGS XF40, $825) 2015
1903-O Small S (NGC G6, $89) (ANACS VF30, $661 - $805) (PCGS XF40, $1,389) 2017
1903-S Micro S (PCGS VF25, $278 - $330) 2017
1904-O Fishhook VAM 4B (NGC MS62, $84)
1921-D Capped R VAM 1B (PCGS AU53)
1921-D Unicorn VAM 1N (NGC MS62)
1921-S Thorn Head VAM 1B-4 (NGC VF30, $41) (NGC XF45 - $35 - $217) (NGC AU58, $200) (PCGS MS64, $376)
*note: there are thousands of VAM error coins available for Morgan dollars.

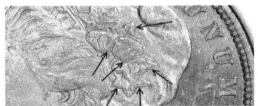
1878 Tripple Bloosoms

1921-1935 1964 Peace Dollar

Above is a 1921 peace dollar

The mint overlapped the design change from the Morgan dollar to the peace design in 1921. Many coin publications purported that a 1964 peace dollar exists but no samples have ever appeared from any sources. The mint must have destroyed all of the mintage after deciding not to issue the coins. Will some of these coins show up like the 1913 V nickel in future? Only time will tell.

Variations and Errors
1922 Extra Hair VAM 2C (ANACS MS63, $85)
1922 Triple Die Reverse VAM 5C (NGC MS62, $80)
1922 Line in Tiara VAM 1A (NGC MS62, $80)
1922 Hair Pin VAM 2F (NGC MS64, $75)
1922 Doubled Motto VAM 4 (NGC MS62, $90)
1922 Tripled Leaves & Eroded Face VAM 5C (NGC MS62, $70)
1922 Scar on Cheek VAM 5A2 (NGC AU58, $200)
1922 Doubled Leaves VAM 6 (NGC MS62, $55)
1922 Moustache VAM 12A (NGC MS62, $160)
1922-D DDO (ANACS AU50, $32) 2015
1922-D DDR (ANACS MS63, $547) 2015
1923 Chin Bar VAM 1F (PCGS MS62, $120) 2015
1923 DDO (NGC MS63, $127) 2015
1923 DDR Leaves (NGC MS62, $78) 2015
1923-D DDR Eagle (NGC AU55, $74) 2015
1925 DDR Shoulder (NGC MS64, $120) 2015
1925-S DDR Leaves (ANCAS AU58, $90) 2015
1926 DDR Leaves (ANACS MS64, $100) 2015
1927-D DDO Trust (PCGS MS65, $4025) 2015
1928-S DDO (ANACS AU55, $100) 2015
1928-S DDO motto (NGC MS63, $635) 20152015
1928-S doubled die "IN GOD WE TRUST" (PCGS MS65, $13,800)

1934-D DDO Motto with large mint mark D (NGC MS63, $441) 2015

1934-D DDO small D mint mark (ANACS VF25, $130) 2015

1971-1978 Eisenhower Dollar

The US Mint decided to place a portrait of President Dwight Eisenhower on a coin after his death to honor the World War II general. The reverse of the coin features the Apollo spacecraft in commemoration of space flight.

The coin was very unpopular from the start of the mintage since it was heavy and bulky to carry. Rarely did this coin circulate freely even though there was a continued mintage from 1971 through 1978. None of these coins carries any significant value. The mint did produce silver clad coins for mint and proof sets until 1978.

Pictured is a 1776-1976 Eisenhower dollar

Variations and Errors

1971 DDO (ANACS MS64, $16) 2015
1971 DDR (ANACS AU55, $15) 2015
1971-S DDR (H, ANACS PR68, $20-$30)
1971-S DDO DDR (ANACS MS65, $35) 2015
1971-S DDR (ANACS PR66, $29) 2015
1972-D DDR (NGC MS66, $250) 2015
1973-S DDO (ANACS MS66, $56) 2015
1977-D struck on silver planchet (NGC MS63, $13,000) 2016

1979-1981 1999 Susan B Anthony

The mint determined that there was a need for a dollar coin to offset the cost of minting dollar bills and the mintage of the Susan B Anthony dollar began in 1979. After only three years of mintage, the mint discovered stock piles of these coins remained in bank vaults and the mint ended production.

No DDO, DDR or RPM coins could be located at auctions. After 18 years, the mint stamped out a 1999 Susan B coin when vending machines and tolls accepted the dollar coin.

Variations and Errors
1979-P wide rim (NCG MS64, $19-$31) (NCG MS65, $42-$44) (NCG MS66, $104-$128) (NCG MS67, $920-$977)
The wide rim and the normal rim coins sell at auction in the same range, making the wide rim version nothing significant.
No date – Struck on a brass cent (PCGS AU58, $3450) -2015
1979-P struck on a quarter planchet (ANACS MS63, $690) 2015
1979-S struck on a cent planchet (PCGS MS64, $5400) 2015
1979-P struck on a quarter planchet (ANACS MS63, $690) 2015
1979-S struck on a cent planchet (PCGS MS64, $5400) 2015

Susan B Anthony minted on a brass planchet

2000- Sacagawea Dollar

Above is a 2000 Sacagawea dollar

The mint dropped the Susan B in favor of a golden colored dollar. Only the 2000, 2001, and the 2012 Sacagawea dollar production was minted for circulation. The dollar mintage has continued every year for proof sets and special rolled issues by the mint. With the 2010 mintages, the reverse of the coin was changed and the date was moved to the rolled edge of the coin. As with many coin issues, dating coins on a rolled edge leads to errors with missing lettering. There has been a new design every year since 2010.

Variations and Errors
2000-P wounded eagle (ANACS MS64, $100) 2017
2000-P struck on a Susan B planchet (PCGS MS66, $8050)
2009 missing letter edging (PCGS MS66, $150) 2014

2007- Presidential dollars

The presidential commemorative dollar series began in 2007 with the issuance of George Washington. With the very first issuance of this series, a number of Washington Presidential dollars appeared without the edge lettering.

95

Variations and Errors

2007 John Adams Double Edge Letters (NGC MS64, $35) (NGC MS65, $50) (NGC MS66, $241-$748) (PCGS MS67, $1,150)

2007 John Adams Missing Letter edge (ANACS MS65, $50)

2007 John Adams Rotated 85 degrees (PCGS MS64, $150) 2016

2007 John Adams Double Edge Lettering (PCGS Uncirculated, $150) 2016

2007 George Washington Missing Edge Lettering (NGC MS65, $30-$56) (NGC MS66, $36-127)

2007 Thomas Jefferson Missing Edge Letters (PCGS MS65, $50) (PCGS MS66, $546-$1,035) (PCGS MS67, $747-$1,495)

2007 James Madison Missing Edge Letters (NGC MS65, $50)

2007 James Madison –double edge lettering (PCGS MS65, $100) 2014

2007-S Thomas Jefferson Double Struck with Rotation (NGC PR69, $460)

2008 Andrew Jackson Missing Edge Letters (PCGS SP67, $153) 2016

2008 James Monroe Missing Edge Letters (PCGS SP66, $300) 2016

2008 John Quincy Adams Missing Edge Letters (PCGS SP66, $49) 2014

2008 Martin Van Buren Missing Edge Letters (NGC MS66, $460) (NGC MS67, $1,265) (NGC MS68, $1,840)

2009-D Zachary Taylor Missing Letter Edge (NGC MS66, $431)

2009 William Henry Harrison Missing Letter Edge (NGC MS66, $432) (NGC MS67, $575-$1,150) (NGC MS69, $1,955)

2009 James K Polk Missing Letter Edge (NGC MS65, $50)

2009 John Tyler Missing Letter Edge (NGC MS67, $505)

2009 Zackery Taylor Missing Letter Edge (NGC MS66, $150) 2016

2010 James Buchanan Missing Letter Edge (PCGS MS66, $170) 2016

2010 Millard Fillmore Missing Letter Edge (NGC MS66, $460)

2012 Cleveland Missing Letter Edge (PCGS MSMS64, $50)

Off-Center Coins 1900 – date
Includes Many Other Error Types

Many error coins' escape detections by the US Mint while most are scrapped. Most dates contain some type of error in all denominations. The listings in this section provide the collector a good over-view of what collectors have paid for specific errors and it represents a good sample for determining a fair value. In some cases, collectors actually have paid more for the same error in lessor grades. This is the only comprehensive collection of errors available.

There is no valid reason why some encapsulations call out "off center" and do not include the off center percentage. In some cases, more is paid for a coin that simply states off center verses with a noted percentage. Some dates and errors have higher prices paid in lower grades making this book a valuable guide for collectors to understand the market.

All coins listed are off center and many with additional errors.

Bonded, Triple Struck Lincoln Cent

97

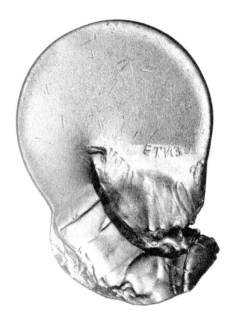

Jefferson Nickel Brockage

Fold Over Strike

98

Saddle Strike

Triple Strike

99

Lincoln Cent Struck on a Dime Planchet

Off Center Undated Lincoln Cents and Other Errors
Indian Cent (MS62, $405 - $1,150) (MS64, $375 - $890)
Lincoln Cent Wheat (MS62, $92) (MS65, $12 -$150) (MS66, $14 - $150)
Lincoln Cent Wheat Brockage (AU58, $82) (MS63, $80)
Lincoln Cent Memorial (MS60, $11 - $35) (MS62, $21 - $130) (MS63, $16) (MS64, $23)
Lincoln Cent Memorial Broadstruck, Brockage (MS64, $26 - $80) (MS65, $7)
Lincoln Cent Memorial Brockage (MS60, $20 - $35) (MS63, $25) (MS64, $15 - $25) (MS65, $22)
Lincoln Cent Memorial Brockage (MS63, $30)
Lincoln Cent Memorial Brockage Die Cap (MS64, $75)
Lincoln Cent Memorial Brockage Strike Through (MS66, $30 - $40)
Lincoln Cent Memorial Brockage Indent (MS64, $115)
Lincoln Cent Struck on Dime Planchet (MS62, $559 - $750)
Lincoln Cent Struck on Dime Saddle Strike (MS63, $33) (MS64, $115)
Lincoln Cent Memorial Double Struck (MS64, $45 - $115) (MS65, $30 - $380)
Lincoln Cent Memorial Double Struck Saddle Struck (MS64, $70) (MS65, $139) (MS66, $49)
Lincoln Cent Memorial Fold Over Strike (MS62, $230 - $460)
Lincoln Cent Memorial Fold Over Strike (MS63, $1,840) (MS64, $650 - $755)
Lincoln Cent Memorial Saddle Struck (MS62, $212) (MS64, $65 - $94) (MS65, $165) (MS66, $445)
Lincoln Cent Memorial Triple Clip (MS66, $155 - $700)
Lincoln Cent Memorial Triple Struck on Silver Dime (MS64, $2,600) (MS66, $650) (MS67, $7,700)
Lincoln Cent Memorial Triple Struck (MS64, $300) (MS65, $405) (MS66, $155)
Lincoln Cent Memorial Type II Ten Cent Planchet (MS64, $1,555) (MS65, $1,555)
Lincoln Cent Memorial Zinc Alloy (MS64, $288) (MS66, $865)

Off Center Undated Nickels and Other Errors
Liberty Nickel (MS60, $863) (MS62, $31 - $900) (MS63, $650)
Liberty Nickel Double Struck (MS64, $4,320)
Buffalo Nickel (MS62, $750 - $1,000) (MS63, $1,265) (MS64, $2,350)
Jefferson Nickel (AU58, $705) (MS60, $16 - $375) (MS63, $15 - $200) (PR63, $69) (MS64, $15 - $205)
Jefferson Nickel Broadstruck (XF45, $150)

Jefferson Nickel Broadstruck (MS65, $7)
Jefferson Nickel Broadstruck, Brockage (MS64, $8
Jefferson Nickel Brockage (MS63, $34) (MS64, $31)
Jefferson Nickel Clad Dime Planchet (MS64, $185)
Jefferson Nickel Clad Planchet (MS64, $1,880)
Jefferson Nickel Clipped Planchet (MS63, $140)
Jefferson Nickel Defective Planchet (MS63, $1060 - $1,100)
Jefferson Nickel Double Curved Clipped Planchet (MS64, $140)
Jefferson Nickel Double Struck (MS60, $30) (MS63, $20 - $565)
(MS64, $75 - $820)
Jefferson Nickel Double Struck Saddle Struck (MS63, $106 -
$345) (MS65, $247)
Jefferson Nickel Double Struck Saddle Struck on a Cent Planchet
(MS64, $1,495)
Jefferson Nickel Double Struck Saddle Struck on a Dime
Planchet (MS64, $823 - $955)
Jefferson Nickel Double Struck Saddle Struck w/Curved Clip
(MS66, $690)
Jefferson Nickel Double Struck Saddle Struck w/Straight Clip
(MS66, $435)
Jefferson Nickel Flip Over Double Strike (MS63, $210) (PR64,
$105)
Jefferson Nickel Multiple Strikes (MS64, $130)
Jefferson Nickel on a Silver Dime Planchet (MS62, $635 - $690)
(MS63, $1,150 - $1,450)
Jefferson Nickel on Silver Dime Planchet Saddle Struck (MS64,
$940 - $1,210)
Jefferson Nickel Quadruple Struck (MS62, $795)
Jefferson Nickel Stretch Strike (MS60, $40)
Jefferson Nickel Struck on a One Cent Planchet (MS60, $244)
(MS63, $245) (MS64, $750 - $980)
Jefferson Nickel Struck on Type One Planchet (MS63, $1,265)
Jefferson Nickel Triple Curved Clipped Planchet (MS64, $150)
Jefferson Nickel Triple Struck (MS62, $165)
Jefferson Nickel Triple Struck, Saddle Struck (MS67, $920)

Off Center Undated Dimes and Other Errors
Barber Dime (MS60, $550)
Mercury Dime (MS63, $2,875)
Roosevelt Dime (MS60, $65) (MS62, $105) (MS63, $21) (MS64,
$138) (MS65 $14) (MS66, $423)
Roosevelt Dime Bonded Multiple Strikes (MS63, $1,450)
Roosevelt Dime Broadstruck, Brockage (MS63, $35) (MS65, $80)
Roosevelt Dime Clad Multiple Struck Bonded (MS65, $1,555)

Roosevelt Dime Double Struck (MS63, $150) (MS64, $127-$575)
Roosevelt Dime Double Struck, Saddle Struck (MS65, $153)
Roosevelt Dime Double Struck 50%/60% (MS64, $1,380)
Roosevelt Dime Missing Reverse Clad Layer (MS63, $376)
Roosevelt Dime Saddle Struck (MS65, $79 - $130)

Off Center Undated Quarters and Other Errors
State Quarter Double Struck (MS65, $1,495)
State Quarter Double Struck Die Cap (MS65, $1,265) (MS67, $650)
Virginia Quarter Straight Clip (MS65, $415)
Washington Quarter (MS60, $74) (MS64, $48) (MS65, $60)
Washington Quarter Double Struck (MS62, $546) (MS63, $70 - $588)
Washington Quarter Double Struck Die Cap (MS65, $1,150)
Washington Quarter on a Cent Planchet (MS65, $999)
Washington Quarter on Silver Dime Planchet (MS62, $245) (MS63, $635)
Washington Quarter Type I Planchet (MS62, $2,185)

Off Center Undated Half Dollars and Other Errors
Walking Liberty Half Double Struck (MS64, $32,900)
Walking Liberty Half Struck on a Steel Cent Planchet (MS64, $30,550 - $44,000)
Franklin Half Struck on a Quarter Planchet (MS65, $7,650) (PR65, $14,100)
Kennedy Half (AU50, $92) (AU55, $300) (AU58, $185 - $1,380) (MS60, $288) (MS62, $253 - $375) (MS63, $825 - $1,150) (MS64, $185 - $415) (MS66, $374) (MS67, $460)
Kennedy Half Brockage (MS64, $4,465)
Kennedy Half Clip (MS65, $735 - $920)
Kennedy Half Double Struck (MS65, $978) (MS66, $1,495)
Kennedy Half Struck on a Cent Planchet (MS62, $4,900)
Kennedy Half Struck on a Quarter Planchet (MS63, $920)
Kennedy Half Type 1 (MS63, $820 - $920)

Off Center Undated Dollars
Morgan Dollar (XF40, $4,000) (AU50, $4,900)
Peace Dollar (MS62, $9,775)
Eisenhower (MS64, $677)
Eisenhower Double Struck (MS62, $2,100)
Susan B (MS64, $3,300) (MS66, $355 - $2000)
Susan B Struck on a Cent Planchet (MS63, $5875)

103

1900

1900 Indian Cent 5%– (VG10, $45) (AU58, $184) (MS64, $435)
1900 Indian Cent 10% – (VF30, $149) (MS63, $375) (MS65, $400)
1990-D Lincoln Cent (MS63, $10)
1900 Liberty Nickel 5% (MS63, $405)
1900 Liberty Nickel 12% (VG30, $325)
1900 Liberty Nickel 50% (XF45, $578 - 635)
1900 Barber Dime 12% (AU50, $460)
1900-S Barber Dime 10% (AU50, $435)
1900 Barber Quarter 10% (AU50, $1,200)
1900 Barber Quarter 15% (VF25, $920)
1900 Barber Half 7% (AU58, $4,370)

1901

1901 Indian Cent 5% – (VF30, $86) (VF35, $65) (AU55, $150)
1901 Indian Cent 10% – 15% (XF45, $160) (AU50, $180) (AU58, $230 - 255)
1901 Indian Cent 15% –25% (VG8, $185) (AU55, $285) (AU58, $290) (AU55, $285) (MS64, $495 - $630) (MS65, $545 - $2,000)
1901 Indian Cent 30% – (VF30, $230) (VF45, $175) (MS63, $400)
1901 Liberty Nickel 5% – (XF45, $240)
1901 Liberty Nickel 10% – (VF35, $210) (XF45, $435) (AU58, $920)
1901 Barber Dime 5% – (AU50, $235) (AU53, $255) (AU58, $375) (MS61, $460)
1901 Barber Dime 20% – (AU58, $1,000)
1901 Barber Quarter 5% – (AU55, $865 - $1,495)
1901 Barber Quarter 10% – (AU58, $4,300)

1902

1902 Indian Cent 5% – (VF20, $66) (VF35, $100 - $150) (MS63, $138) (AU58, $160) (MS62, $205)
1902 Indian Cent 10% – (VG8, $110 - $125) (XF40, $230) (MS60, $140) (MS63, $365 - $435)
1902 Indian Cent 12% – (F15, $160) (XF40, $255)
1902 Indian Cent 15% – (AU50, $90) (MS64, $365 - $455)
1902 Indian Cent 17% – (AU58, $230)
1902 Indian Cent 20% – (MS65, $805)
1902 Indian Cent 30% – (VG8, $115 -$150)
1902 Indian Cent 35% – (VG8, $230) (MS63, $720)
1902 Indian Cent 45% – (AU55, $800) (AU58, $645)
1902 Liberty Nickel 7% – (F15, $205)
1902 Liberty Nickel 10% – (VF30, $205)

1902 Barber Dime 10% – (AU58, $635)
1902-S Morgan Dollar 5% – (XF45, $575)

1903
1903 Indian Cent 5% - (F12, $66) (MS62, $230)
1903 Indian Cent 10% - (XF40, $200 - $225) (AU58, $276)
1903 Indian Cent 12% - (VF20, $130) (AU55, $260)
1903 Indian Cent 15% - (MS63, $300 - $425) (MS64, $635)
(MS65, $635)
1903 Indian Cent 20% - (AU58, $185) (AU55, $322)
1903 Indian Cent 30% - (XF45, $276 - $375)
1903 Indian Cent 65% Struck Twice- (MS62, $920)
1903 Liberty Nickel 20% - (AU58 - $885 - $1500)
1903 Liberty Nickel 65% - (MS64 - $2,875)
1903 Barber Dime 3% – (XF45, $195)
1903 Barber Dime 5% – (AU58, $150)
1903 Barber Dime 40% Brockage – (AU58, $1,380)

1904
1904 Indian Cent 3% - (F15, $29)
1904 Indian Cent 5% - (MS63, $207)
1904 Indian Cent 7% - (F12, $66)
1904 Indian Cent 10% - (AU58, $140) (MS63, $460) (MS64,
$425)
1904 Indian Cent 15% - (XF45, $175) (AU53, $185)
1904 Indian Cent 20% - Double Struck (MS60, $1,150)
1904 Indian Cent 25% - (AU55, $345 - $489)904 Indian Cent
30% - Double Struck - (XF45, $690 - $1,880)
1904 Indian Cent 65% - Double Struck - (F12, $632) (MS62,
$2,300)
1904 Indian Cent 95% - Double Struck - (VG10, $188)
1904 Indian Cent Double Struck with Brockage – (MS62, $1,125)
1904 Barber Dime10% - (AU50, $375) (MS63, $635)
1904 Barber Dime 20% - (AU58, $1,090)
1904 Barber Dime Flip Over - (XF45, $4.025)

Above is a 1904 Indian Cent Double Struck 30%

1905
1905 Indian Cent 5% - (MS64, $276) (MS65, $375)
1905 Indian Cent 7% - (F12, $75)
1905 Indian Cent 10% - (AU50, $150) (AU53, $195) (AU55, $160) (MS64, $253)
1905 Indian Cent 10% With Ragged Clip - (XF45, $211)
1905 Indian Cent 12% - 15% (AU58, $300) (MS63, $376 - $515)
1905 Indian Cent 20% - 25% - (AU55, $230) (AU58, $288) (MS63, $253 - $520)
1905 Indian Cent 35% - (VF20, $255)
1905 Indian Cent 40% - (MS64, $1,035)
1905 Indian Cent 85% Chain Struck Edge - (MS64, $1,175)
1905 Indian Cent Struck on Quarter Eagle Planchet (MS64, $253,000)
1905 Liberty Nickel 10% - (AG3 - $104)
1905 Barber Dime 5% - (AU58, $460)

1906
1906 Indian Cent 10% - (G6, $135) (MS63, $350 - $430) (MS64, $400)
1906 Indian Cent 15% - (AU58, $205 - $255)
1906 Indian Cent 35% - (MS63, $690 - $1,265)
1906 Indian Cent 60% - (VG6, $255)
1906 Liberty Nickel 10% - (AU58 - $184)

1906 Liberty Nickel 12% - (AU55 - $404) (AU55, $635)
1906 Liberty Nickel 35% - (MS64 - $2,760)
1906 Barber Dime 5% - (AU50, $375) (MS60, $175)
1906 Barber Dime 10% - MS61, $635)
1906-D Half Dollar 3% - (MS61, $1,050) (AU58, $2,185)

1907
1907 Indian Cent 5% - (VF35, $69) (AU55, $127)
1907 Indian Cent 7% - (XF45, $127)
1907 Indian Cent 10% - (MS64, $865)
1907 Indian Cent 15% - (AU53, $206) (VF30, $376) (MS63, $1,300)
1907 Indian Cent 22% - (XF45, $311)
1907 Indian Cent 25% - (MS64, $520)
1907 Indian Cent 35% - (AU58, $435) (MS63, $1,265)
1907 Indian Cent 50% - (MS64, $1,100)
1907 Indian Cent 50% Double Struck- (VF30, $745 - $1,300)
1907 Liberty Nickel 5% - (MS62 - $325) (MS62, $375)
1907 Liberty Nickel 10% - (VF20 - $145)
1907 Liberty Nickel 15% - (VF20 - $360) (MS61, $690 - $1,050)
1907 Liberty Nickel 20% - (MS63 - $1,525)
1907 Liberty Nickel 25% - (MS63 - $2,760)
1907 Liberty Nickel 85% Double Struck- (AU50 - $940)
1907 Barber Dime 10% - (AU55, $475 - $605) (PR63, $460)
1907 Barber Dime 20% - (MS62, $605 - $850)
1907-D Barber Dime 20% - (AU55, $835 - $1,225)

1908
1908 Indian Cent 5% - (XF45, $75 - $130) (AU55, $150) (MS64, $355) (MS65, $375 - $555)
1908 Indian Cent 10% - (AU58, $305)
1908 Indian Cent 15% - (VF20, $150) (XF40, $185) (AU53, $196) (MS64, $603)
1908 Indian Cent 20% - (F15, $150) (MS62, $345) (MS64, $345)
1908 Indian Cent 25% Double Struck- (XF45, $1,998)
1908 Indian Cent 35% - (VF15, $300) (MS64, $1,035 - $1,725)
1908 Indian Cent 55% - (MS62, $1,100)
1908 Indian Cent 90% Double Struck- (VF30, $805) (XF40, $605)
1908-D Barber Dime 5% - (XF40, $196) (AU50, $150)

1909
1909 Lincoln Cent 50% - (MS67, $44)
1909 Barber Dime Broad struck – (AU55, $184)

1910

1910 Lincoln Cent 5% - (XF45, $115 - $130)
1910 Lincoln Cent 10% - (XF45, $125)
1910 Lincoln Cent 15% Double Struck- (AU58, $405 - $805)
1910 Liberty Nickel 5% - (MS60, $306)
1910 Liberty Nickel 10% - (MS60, $235)

1911

1911 Lincoln Cent 5% - (XF45, $69 - $127)
1911 Lincoln Cent 10% - (VF25, $242)
1911 Lincoln Cent Double Struck - (XF45, $258)
1911 Liberty Nickel 5% - (VF30, $150)
1911 Liberty Nickel 10% - (VF20, $156)
1911 Barber Dime 10% - (AU50, $194
1911-D Barber Dime 5% - (AU50, $184)

1912

1912 Lincoln Cent 10% Double Struck- (AU53, $435)
1912 Lincoln Cent 20% - (AU53, $405) (AU58, $196)
1912-D Lincoln Cent 30% - (MS63, $242)
1912 Liberty Nickel 10% - (G6, $156 - $235) (VF30, $155)
(AU58, $374)
1912-D Liberty Nickel 7% - (AU55, $1,300)
1912-D Liberty Nickel 10% - (AU50, $690)
1912-S Barber Dime 5% - (AU50, $176 - $375)
1912-S Barber Dime 20% - (VF25, $920 - $1,495)

1913

1913 Lincoln Cent 5% - (MS63, $345 - $550)
1913 Lincoln Cent 10% - (MS60, $110)
1913-D Lincoln Cent 10% - (AU55, $145) (MS60, $145)
1913-S Lincoln Cent 5% - (AU55, $435)
1913-S Lincoln Cent 15% - (MS61, $825)
1913 Buffalo Nickel Type I 10% – (AU58, $240) (MS64, $805 - $865)
1913 Buffalo Nickel Struck on a Dime Planchet – (MS66, $46,000)
1913-D Buffalo Nickel Broadstruck – (VF25, $405)
1913-D Buffalo Nickel Type I 5% – (VF30, $81)
1913-D Buffalo Nickel Type I 15% – (VF20, $895)
1913-S Buffalo Nickel Broadstruck – (F15, $200)
1913-S Buffalo Nickel Type I 5% – (MS64, $920)
1913-S Buffalo Nickel Type II 5% – (MS64, $865 - $1,100)
1913 Barber Dime 10% - (AU50, $235) (AU58, $520)
1913 Barber Dime 15% - (AU50, $435)

1914
1914 Lincoln Cent 5% - (XF45, $66 - $185)
1914 Lincoln Cent 10% - (MS60, $105) (MS64, $322)
1914-D Barber Dime 5% (MS61, $247)
1914-D Barber Dime 10% (VG10, $167)
1914-D Barber Dime Broadstruck (MS64, $547)

1915
1915 Lincoln Cent 10% - (F15, $69)
1915-D Lincoln Cent 10% - (F15, $345) (MS62, $259 - $489)
(MS63, $230) (MS64, $288)
1915-S Lincoln Cent AU50, $765)
1915-S Buffalo Nickel (XF45, $506)

1916
1916 Lincoln Cent Broadstruck - (MS63, $104 -$299)
1916-D Lincoln Cent (MS61, $150) (MS63, $207) (MS64, $235)
1916-D Lincoln Cent Broadstruck - (MS64, $575)
1916-D Lincoln Cent 5% (MS65, $345 - 435)
1916-D Lincoln Cent 15% (MS63, $210 - $690) (MS65, $550)
1916-S Lincoln Cent 10% - 12% (MS64, $210)
1916-S Lincoln Cent 20% (MS65, $633)
1916-S Lincoln Cent Broadstruck - (MS63, $145)
1916 Buffalo Nickel (AU55, $662) (MS63, $1,090) (MS64, $2,000)
1916 Buffalo Nickel 5% - (XF45, $300)
1916 Buffalo Nickel 10% - (MS65, $805)
1916 Buffalo Nickel 35% - (MS65, $1,450)
1916-D Buffalo Nickel 5% - (AU55, $345)
1916-D Buffalo Nickel 10% - (G[27] $276)
1916-D Buffalo Nickel 15% - (MS64, $489)
1916-S Buffalo Nickel (MS62, $1,265)
1916-S Buffalo Nickel 10% - (MS62, $588) (MS64, $940)
1916 Barber Dime 20% - (AU58, $690)
1916-S Barber Dime AU50, $110 - $450)
1916-S Barber Dime 3% - 5% - (AU58, $185 - $253) (AU58, $220)
1916-S Barber Dime 7% - (AU55, $1,150)
1916-S Barber Dime 10% - (MS61, $500 - $575)
1916-S Barber Dime 15% - (AU50, $605) (MS62, $586)
1916-S Barber Dime Broadstruck (MS65, $1,150)
1916-S Mercury Dime (XF45, $58 - $207) (MS60, $282)

---

[27] G - Genuine

109

1917

1917 Lincoln Cent (MS64, $127)
1917 Lincoln Cent 5% - (MS64, $105)
1917 Lincoln Cent 10% - (MS64, $357) (MS65, $282)
1917 Lincoln Cent 15% - (G4, $47 - $55) (VF20, $56) (AU58, $253 - $920)
1917 Lincoln Cent 20% - (MS63, $126)
1917 Lincoln Cent Broadstruck (MS63, $184)
1917-D Lincoln Cent 5% - (VG8, $52)
1917-D Lincoln Cent 10% - (MS64, $235)
1917-D Lincoln Cent 20% - (MS64, $253)
1917-D Lincoln Cent 15% - (MS63, $208 - $403)
1917-D Lincoln Cent 25% - (XF40, $242)
1917-D Lincoln Cent 35% - (VF30, $161) (MS60, $167)
1917-S Lincoln Cent (XF45, $75) (MS61, $276)
1917-S Lincoln Cent 5% - (MS64, $104)
1917-S Lincoln Cent 10% - (AU50, $110 - $173) (AU55, $127) (MS62, $207)
1917-S Lincoln Cent 20% - (VF20, $130 - $150) (XF45, $197) (AU58, $220)
1917-S Lincoln Cent 25% - (MS63, $547)
1917-S Lincoln Cent 45% - (AU50, $196 - $805)
1917-S Lincoln Cent 55% - (MS64, $576)
1917-S Lincoln Cent 60% - (AU55, $276)
1917 Mercury Dime (AU58, $403)
1917 Buffalo Nickel (AU58, $863)
1917 Buffalo Nickel 15% (VF35, $494)
1917 Buffalo Nickel 25% (AU55, $564 - $1,725) (AU58, $647)
1917 Buffalo Nickel 45% (MS64, $2,990)
1917-S Buffalo Nickel 20% (AU58, $1,763)
1917-S Buffalo Nickel Broadstruck (MS64, $1,725)
1917 Mercury Dime 5% - (AU53, $150)
1917 Mercury Dime 15% - (MS63, $220)
1917 Mercury Dime 25% - (MS64, $460 - $489)
1917-S Mercury Dime 15% - (AU58, $322)
1917-S Standing Liberty Quarter – 10% (AU55, $8,050)

1918

1918 Lincoln Cent (AU55, $48) (AU58, $69 - $149) (MS64, $299)
1918 Lincoln Cent 5% (F12, $21)
1918 Lincoln Cent 35% (VF30, $127 - $196)
1918 Lincoln Cent Double Struck 55% (MS65, $1,725)
1918 Lincoln Cent Double Struck 85 % (AU58, $748)
1918 Lincoln Cent Struck Nine Times (F15, $2,100)

1918-D Lincoln Cent 5% (MS61, $150) (MS62, $99- $173)
(MS64, $805)
1918-D Lincoln Cent 10% (MS61, $92)
1918-S Lincoln Cent (MS62, $348)
1918-S Lincoln Cent 12% (VF20, $133)
1918-S Lincoln Cent 15% (AU50, $161) (AU50, $202 - $223)
1918-S Lincoln Cent 30% (AU58, $311)
1918-S Lincoln Cent 35% (MS60, $243 - $374)
1918-S Lincoln Cent 40% (MS64, $403)
1918-S Lincoln Cent 50% (MS62, $432 - $764)
1918 Buffalo Nickel (XF40, $414)
1918 Buffalo Nickel 5% (MS64, $725)
1918 Buffalo Nickel 15% (AU50, $282)
1918 Buffalo Nickel 20% (XF40, $863 - $1,495)
1918 Buffalo Nickel 25% (AU53, $2,300) (AU58, $1,925)
1918-D Buffalo Nickel 10% (MS64, $1,725 - $1,897)
1918-D Buffalo Nickel 12% (MS63, $1,208)
1918-D Buffalo Nickel 15% (MS63, $2,999)
1918-S Buffalo Nickel (MS64, $8,625)
1918-S Buffalo Nickel 25% (AU58, $940)
1918-D Mercury Dime 35% (AU58, $863)
1918-S Standing Liberty Quarter 5% (MS64, $8,338)
1918-S Standing Liberty Quarter 10% (MS63, $5,570)
1918-S Standing Liberty Quarter 13% (MS63, $9,488)
1918-S Half Dollar 5% (PCGS AU50, $2,875)
1918-S Half Dollar 10% (PCGS MS64, $11,500) (PCGS MS65,
$10,575)

111

Above is a 1918 Buffalo Nickel 40%

1919
1919 Lincoln Cent (AU50, $42) (MS62, $64 -$265) (MS63, $66 -
$218) (MS64, $92 - $161)
1919 Lincoln Cent 5% (MS63, $150)
1919 Lincoln Cent 10% (MS61, $184) (MS64, $92)
1919 Lincoln Cent 15% (MS63, $115)
1919 Lincoln Cent 20% (MS62, $138) (MS63, $200)
1919 Lincoln Cent 25% (MS63, $1,410)
1919 Lincoln Cent 40% (MS62, $253)
1919 Lincoln Cent Broad Struck (MS64, $299)
1919-D Lincoln Cent (AU50, $35)
1919-D Lincoln Cent 15% (AU55, $299)
1919-S Lincoln Cent (VG10, $51) (F12, $58) (VF20, $25 -$45)
(XF45, $46) (AU58, $86)
1919-S Lincoln Cent 5% (AU55, $56 - $161)
1919-S Lincoln Cent 10% (VF35, $99) (MS64, $299)
1919-S Lincoln Cent 15% (MS63, $92 - $150) (MS64, $588)
1919-S Lincoln Cent 20% (F12, $84) (MS60, $141) (MS63, $300)
1919-S Lincoln Cent 30% (MS65, $520)
1919-S Lincoln Cent 35% (MS63, $647)
1919-S Lincoln Cent 45% (AU55, $230)
1919-S Lincoln Cent 75% (AU55, $374)
1919-x Buffalo Nickel 15% (MS64, $1,035) (MS65, $862)

1919 Buffalo Nickel (AU55, $547) (MS63, $863) (MS64, $834)
1919 Buffalo Nickel 5% (XF45, $345) (MS61, $470) (MS65, $690 - $1,150)
1919 Buffalo Nickel 10% (MS63, $187 - $460) (MS64, $1,092) (MS65, $920 - $1,265)
1919 Buffalo Nickel 12% (AU58, $1,150)
1919 Buffalo Nickel 15% (MS63, $460 - $978) (MS64, $1,092)
1919 Buffalo Nickel 20% (MS64, $978) (MS65, $1,410)
1919 Buffalo Nickel Broad Struck (AU53, $161)
1919-D Buffalo Nickel 5% (MS64, $2,128 - $2,990)
1919-S Buffalo Nickel 15% (MS60, $662)
1919 Mercury Dime (AU53, $207)
1919 Mercury Dime 5% (AU53, $207)
1919 Mercury Dime 10% (AU58, $219) (MS62, $305)
1919-D Mercury Dime 5% (AU55, $219)
1919-D Mercury Dime 20% (MS63, $748)
1919 Standing Liberty Quarter 5% (MS64, $1,880)
1919 Standing Liberty Quarter 15% (MS63, $8,625)
1919 Standing Liberty Quarter 50% (XF45, $15,525)

1920

1920 Lincoln Cent (VF20, $60) (XF45, $45) (AU55, $69)
1920 Lincoln Cent 10% (MS64, $64)
1920 Lincoln Cent 20% (XF45, $50) (MS64, $150-$345) (MS65, $288)
1920 Lincoln Cent 30% (MS63, $360)
1920 Lincoln Cent 40% (XF40, $161) (MS64, $374)
1920 Lincoln Cent 40% with Brockage (VG10, $633)
1920 Lincoln Cent Broadstruck (AU55, $71)
1920-D Lincoln Cent (AU55, $207)
1920-S Lincoln Cent 20% (MS64, $423)
1920-S Lincoln Cent 40% (XF45, $423)
1920 Buffalo Nickel (XF45, $414) (AU50, $403 - $460) (MS63, $920)
1920 Buffalo Nickel 5% (AU58, $306)
1920 Buffalo Nickel 7% (AU53, $432) (MS63, $690)
1920 Buffalo Nickel 10% (MS64, $748)
1920 Buffalo Nickel 12% (MS63, $882) (MS65, $1,093)
1920 Buffalo Nickel 15% (XF45, $178) (MS60, $220) (MS62, $541 - $705) (MS63, $633) (MS64, $805)
1920 Buffalo Nickel 20% (AU58, $604 - $738) (MS63, $423 - $1,265)
1920 Buffalo Nickel 30% (F12, $863) (AU50, $1,058) (AU58, $1,150) (MS62, $940 - $1,093)
1920 Buffalo Nickel 35% (VF25, $460)
1920 Buffalo Nickel 40% (AU55, $1,058)
1920 Buffalo Nickel Broadstruck (MS66, $1,035)
1920 Buffalo Struck on One Cent (XF40, $1,998)
1920 Buffalo Struck on One Cent 40% (MS64, $12,338)
1920-x Buffalo Nickel (XF40, $414)
1920-x Buffalo Nickel 15% (MS62, $892) (MS64, $805)
1920-x Buffalo Nickel 20% (MS62, $863)
1920-x Buffalo Nickel 25% (XF45, $978)
1920-x Buffalo Nickel 35% (VF45, $437) (AU58, $1,380)
1920-x Buffalo Nickel 40% (MS64, $17,250)
1920-x Buffalo Nickel 60% (AU58, $1,880)
1920-x Buffalo Nickel 65% (MS64, $2,530)
1920-x Buffalo Nickel 75% (MS63, $2,070)
1920-D Buffalo Nickel 10% (XF45, $282) (AU50, $322)
1920-S Buffalo Nickel 3% (MS64, $1,840)
1920-S Buffalo Nickel 10% (MS63, $4,888)
1920-S Buffalo Nickel 80% Double Struck (AU55, $8,050)
1920 Mercury Dime 20% (MS64, $460)
1920 Mercury Dime 40% (MS63, $2,990)

1920-D Mercury Dime 10% (AU55, $242) (MS62, $374 - $999) (MS63, $676)
1920-D Mercury Dime 13% (MS64, $940 - $1,116)
1920-S Mercury Dime (MS62, $920)

1921
1921 Lincoln Cent 5% (MS64, $202)
1921 Lincoln Cent 10% (VG8, $78) (MS62, $207)
1921 Buffalo Nickel 7% (MS61, $690)
1921-x Buffalo Nickel 45% (MS63, $2,300)
1921 Mercury Dime 10% (AU55, $863)
1921 Mercury Dime 15% (NGC, $1,175)
1921 Morgan Dollar 3% (AU50, $863) (MS64, $264 - $385)
1921 Morgan Dollar 5% (MS63, $1,668)
1921 Morgan Dollar 8% (XF45, $1,410)
1921-D Morgan Dollar 5% (AU50, $3,220)
1921-D Morgan Dollar 7% (AU50, $1,265)
1921-D Morgan Dollar 13% (AU58, $8,050)
1921-S Morgan Dollar 5% (AU55, $2,588 - $3,055) (AU58, $1,175 - $1,845)
1921-S Morgan Dollar 25% (MS62, $14,375)
1921-S Morgan Dollar Double Struck (AU58, $11,500)

1922
1922 Lincoln Cent 10% (XF40, $4,313 - $5,290)
1922-S Peace Dollar 5% (MS62, $5,175)
1922-S Peace Dollar 15% (MS65, $39,657)

1923
1923-S Liberty Quarter 25% (AU58, $10,925)
1923-S Peace Dollar 5% (AU50, $5,320)

1924
1924 Lincoln Cent (MS65, $80)
1924-S Lincoln Cent 25% (AU50, $276 - $547)
1924-S Lincoln Cent 30% (AU50, $376) (MS62, $705) (MS65, $1,765)
1924 Buffalo Nickel 35% (XF40, $633)
19xx Buffalo Nickel 75% (MS63, $1,265)
1924 Mercury Dime 15% (MS64, $1,122)
1924-S Standing Liberty Quarter 10% (XF45, $4,485)
1924-S Standing Liberty Quarter 15% (XF45, $3,795)

1925
1925-D Lincoln Cent (AU50, $161)
1925 Buffalo Nickel 5% (MS63, $633) (MS64, $575)
1925 Buffalo Nickel 20% (MS64, $863)
1925-D Buffalo Nickel 25% (XF45, $978)

1926
1926-D Lincoln Cent 5% (VF25, $64) (MS64, $288)
1926-D Lincoln Cent 10% (F15, $59)
1926-x Buffalo Nickel 40% (MS63, $2,585)

1927

1928
1928-D Lincoln Cent (XF45, $63 - $99)
1928 Buffalo Nickel 15% (VF30, $404)
1928-S Buffalo Nickel 10% (AU58, $748)
1928-S Mercury Dime 15% (MS62, $432 - $540) (MS63, $402)
(MS64, $635 - $718) (MS65, $546 - $978)

1929
1929-D Lincoln Cent (MS63, $431)
1929-S Lincoln Cent 15% (MS66, $647)
1929 Buffalo Nickel 5% (MS64, $633)
1929 Buffalo Nickel 20% (XF45, $978)
1929-S Buffalo Nickel 5% (AU58, $633)
1929-S Buffalo Nickel 10% (AU58, $546)
1929-x Buffalo Nickel 40% (MS64, $2,588)
1929-S Mercury Dime (MS60, $115)
1929-S Mercury Dime 10% (AU58, $253)
1929-S Mercury Dime 12% (AU55, $276)
1929-S Mercury Dime 15% (MS62 FB, $489)
1929-S Liberty Quarter Broadstruck (MS62, $2,818 - $2,875)

1930
1930-D Lincoln Cent 10% (MS62, $74)

1931

1932
1932 Washington Quarter 50% (MS63, $518)

1933

1934
1934 Lincoln Cent 10% (VG10, $50)
1934 Buffalo Nickel (XF40, $184)
1934 Buffalo Nickel 10% (MS64, $589)
1934-D Mercury Dime 5% (MS60, $173)
1934-D Mercury Dime 12% (AU55, $232)

1935
1935 Buffalo Nickel (AU50, $196 - $276) (MS60, $230 - $382)
1935 Buffalo Nickel 5% (AU58, $299 - $518) (MS60, $282 - $345) (MS63, $470) (MS64, $259 - $690)
1935 Buffalo Nickel 7% (MS63, $617)
1935 Buffalo Nickel 10% (AU58, $374 - $529) (MS62, $253 - $805) (MS63, $547- $1,305) (MS64, $517)
1935 Buffalo Nickel 12% (MS63, $805)
1935 Buffalo Nickel 15% (MS65, $1,380)
1935 Buffalo Nickel 20% (AU53, $604) (MS65, $1,265)
1935 Buffalo Nickel 25% (MS62, $2,760)
1935-x Buffalo Nickel 10% (MS64, $547)
1935-x Buffalo Nickel 20% (MS62, $1,725)
1935 Mercury Dime 20% (MS63, $460)

1936
1936 Lincoln Cent 5% (MS64, $121)
1936 Lincoln Cent Broadstruck (MS62, $690) (MS65, $87)
1936 Buffalo Nickel (AU50, $120 - $184) (MS60, $499)
1936 Buffalo Nickel 5% (AU58, $207 - $306) (MS60, $173) (MS62, $253 - $518) (MS63, $235 - $705) (MS64, $340)
1936 Buffalo Nickel 7% (MS63, $282 - $805)
1936 Buffalo Nickel 10% (VF25, $220) (AU55, $529) (AU58, $374 - $438) (MS60, $138) (MS63, $617) (MS64, $220 - $764) (MS65, $437)
1936 Buffalo Nickel 12% (AU58, $529)
1936 Buffalo Nickel 15% (AU58, $220) (MS63, $604 - $823) (MS64, $863)
1936 Buffalo Nickel Broadstruck (MS62, $150 - $345)
1936-x Buffalo Nickel 15% (MS62, $547 - $805) (MS63, $575 - $920)
1936 Mercury Dime 10% (VF30, $149)
1936 Mercury Dime 20% (MS61, $345)

1937
1937 Lincoln Cent (VF20, $161)
1937 Lincoln Cent 15% (MS64, $95 - $150)

1937 Buffalo Nickel (VF30, $184) (AU50, $153) (MS61, $31) (MS63, $350- $375)
1937 Buffalo Nickel 5% (MS62, $322) (MS63, $285 - $538)
1937 Buffalo Nickel 10% (MS62, $418) (MS64, $575) (MS65, $862 - $1,035) (MS66, $588 - $1,175)
1937 Buffalo Nickel 15% (AU58, $220) (MS63, $705 - $1,610)
1937 Buffalo Nickel 20% (MS62, $705)

1938

1939
1939 Lincoln Cent (AU50, $65)
1939 Lincoln Cent 10% (MS62, $127)
1939 Lincoln Cent 15% (MS64, $207)
1939 Jefferson Nickel 15% (MS64, $230) (MS65, $188 - $219)

1940
1940-S Lincoln Cent (MS60, $69) (MS62, $161)
1940-S Lincoln Cent 80% (MS63, $161)
1940-S Jefferson Nickel 5% (AU55, $69)
1940-S Jefferson Nickel 55% (MS66, $547)
1940 Jefferson Nickel 15% (MS64, $219)
1940 Mercury Dime (AU58, $81) (MS61, $207)
1940 Mercury Dime 10% (MS60, $130)

1941
1941 Lincoln Cent (MS65, $37)
1941 Lincoln Cent Broadstruck (MS60, $127)
1941 Lincoln Cent Double Struck 15% (MS64, $412)
1941 Jefferson Nickel (MS62, $11) (MS64, $173)
1941 Jefferson Nickel 10% (AU58, $128)
1941 Jefferson Nickel 15% (MS65, $235 - $374)
1941-S Jefferson Nickel (AU50, $24)
1941 Mercury Dime (MS61, $138)
1941 Mercury Dime 15% (MS66, $282)
1941 Mercury Dime 45% (MS62, $940)
1941 Mercury Dime 50% (MS63, $403)
1941 Mercury Dime 80% (AU55, $1,265)
1941-S Mercury Dime (AU58, $110 - $138) (MS62, $75 - $89) (MS64, $121)
1941-S Mercury Dime 10% (MS62, $79)
1941 Walking Liberty Half Mated Pair (AU58, $24,675)

1942
1942 Lincoln Cent (MS60, $27) (MS63, $35)
1942 Lincoln Cent 10% (MS66, $92)
1942 Lincoln Cent 20% (AU58, $69)
1942 Lincoln Cent 40% (MS62, $2,585)
1942 Jefferson Nickel Wartime Issue 40% (MS62, $1,410)
(MS64, $1,559)
1942 Mercury Dime (MS60, $51)
1942 Mercury Dime 30% (MS62, $489)
1942-D Mercury Dime 12% (MS62, $184 - $489)
1942-S Mercury Dime 10% (MS63, $196)
1942-S Mercury Dime 30% (MS60, $1,092)
1942 Walking Liberty Half Broadstruck (MS60, $690)
1942 Walking Liberty Half Struck on A Quarter Planchet (AU58,
$13,800) (MS65, $17,625)

1943
1943 Lincoln Cent (AU55, $276) (AU58, $69) (MS60, $54)
(MS63, $104)
1943 Lincoln Cent 5% (AU50, $42 - $92) (AU58, $130) (MS63,
$165 - $212) (MS64, $74 - $242)
1943 Lincoln Cent 10% (AU55, $55) (MS61, $353) (MS62, $130)
(MS64, $127)
1943 Lincoln Cent 15% (MS65, $432)
1943 Lincoln Cent 20% (MS62, $276)
1943 Lincoln Cent 40% (MS62, $1,035 - $1,410)
1943 Lincoln Cent 75% (MS64, $299)
1943 Lincoln Cent Double Struck 80% (MS64, $1,763)
1943 Lincoln Cent Double Struck 90% (MS61, $604)
1943 Lincoln Cent Struck on a Dime Planchet (MS62, $5,175)
1943-D Lincoln Cent 10% (AU50, $84)
1943-D Lincoln Cent 15% (MS67, $1,610 - $1,998)
1943-S Lincoln Cent (F12, $46) (VF20, $31) (VF30, $54) (XF40,
$19 - $75) (MS60, $42 -$81) (MS64, $81)
1943-S Lincoln Cent 3% (XF20, $41) (AU58, $104) (MS64, $84)
1943-S Lincoln Cent 5% (MS63, $184) (MS64, $218 - $423)
1943-S Lincoln Cent 10% (MS62, $219) (MS63, $460) (MS64,
$259)
1943-S Lincoln Cent 12% (MS62, $253)
1943-S Lincoln Cent 15% (AU58, $104) (MS62, $230 - $441)
(MS66, $374)
1943-S Lincoln Cent Struck on a Dime Planchet (AU58, $4,465)
1943-S Lincoln Cent Struck on a Dime Planchet 15 % (AU55,
$6,757)
1943-x Lincoln Cent 75% (MS64, $299)

1943 Jefferson Nickel (MS64, $51)
1943 Jefferson Nickel Struck on a Steel Planchet (AU55, $2,938)
1943 Mercury Dime 5% (MS62, $138)
1943 Mercury Dime 10% (MS63, $161)
1943-S Mercury Dime (AU50, $133)
1943-S Mercury Dime 10% (MS62, $195)
1943-S Mercury Dime 12% (MS63, $207)
1943-S Mercury Dime 15% (XF40, $104 - $138) (MS60, $44)

1944
1944 Lincoln Cent (XF40, $12) (AU50, $10 - $24) (AU53, $11)
(AU58, $18-$30) (MS62, $45) (MS63, $31) (MS64, $25 - $144)
(MS65, $66)
1944 Lincoln Cent 5% (AU55, $58) (MS63, $69) (MS64, $33-$42)
1944 Lincoln Cent 10% (MS64, $118 - $161)
1944 Lincoln Cent 15% (MS64, $92)
1944 Lincoln Cent 25% (MS64, $165)
1944 Lincoln Cent Double Struck 10% (MS63, $588)
1944-D D/S Lincoln Cent 10% (MS63, $207)
1944-S Lincoln Cent 10% (MS64, $69)
1944-S Lincoln Cent 15% (MS65, $79)
1944-S Lincoln Cent Double Struck 60% (MS60, $329)
1944-P Jefferson Nickel 10% (MS63, $77) (MS64 FS, $1,057)
1944-P Jefferson Nickel 70 % (AU50, $276)
1944 Mercury Dime 5% (AU58, $99) (MS62, $173) (MS64, $188)
(MS65, $104 - $161)
1944 Mercury Dime 10% (AU55, $184) (AU58, $62 - $87) (MS64,
$173 - $230) (MS65, $138)
1944 Mercury Dime 15% (MS64, $167 - $253)
1944 Mercury Dime 20% (MS64, $517) (MS65, $403) (MS65 FB,
$420)
1944 Mercury Dime 30% (MS64, $1,116)
1944 Mercury Dime 35% (MS61, $460)
1944 Mercury Dime 40% (MS63, $805)
1944 Mercury Dime (MS65, $190)
1944 Mercury Dime Broadstruck (MS63, $92 - $115)
1944-D Mercury Dime (AU58, $218)
1944-D Mercury Dime 5% (MS62, $136)
1944-S Mercury Dime (MS60, $104)
1944 Walking Liberty Half 40% (VF20, $1,320)

1945
1945 Lincoln Cent (XF40, $57) (MS60, $11) (MS63, $34) (MS64,
$44 - $92)
1945 Lincoln Cent 10% (MS65, $57) (MS67, $173 - $300)

1945 Lincoln Cent 20% (MS60, $61) (MS63, $92)
1945 Lincoln Cent 25% (XF45, $92)
1945 Lincoln Cent Broadstruck (MS63, $92) (MS65, $31)
1945-D Lincoln Cent (MS64, $42)
1945-S Lincoln Cent 5% (MS62, $50)
1945-S Lincoln Cent 10% (AU53, $87)
1945-P Jefferson Nickel 5% (AU50, $40) (MS65 FS, $138 - $288)
1945-P Jefferson Nickel Broadstruck (MS62, $805)
1945-S Jefferson Nickel 10% (AU55, $163)
1945 Mercury Dime 5% (MS64, $1,840)
1945 Mercury Dime 10% (MS62, $253)
1945 Mercury Dime 12% (MS63, $81)
1945 Mercury Dime 20% (MS64, $999)
1945 Mercury Dime (VF30, $81) (AU55, $127) (MS60, $117 - $212)
1945 Mercury Dime Broadstruck (AU50, $196)
1945-D Mercury Dime 10% (MS62, $253)
1945-D Mercury Dime Broadstruck (MS64, $127)
1945-S Mercury Dime (AU50, $38) (MS63, $115)
1945-x Mercury Dime 20% (MS63, $460)
1945-x Mercury Dime 50% (MS66, $1,495)
1945-S Micro s Mercury Dime (AU58, $230)
1945-S Walking Liberty Half Dollar (MS63, $41,125)

1946
1946 Lincoln Cent 10% (MS66, $149)
1946-S Lincoln Cent (AU58, $17 - $87)
1946-S Lincoln Cent 40% (MS66, $259)
1946 Roosevelt Dime 60% (MS64, $127)

1947
1947-S Lincoln Cent 15% (MS61, $156)

1948
1948-S Jefferson Nickel 15% (MS64 FS, $329 - $391)
1948-S Roosevelt Dime (AU55, $172 - $219)

1949
1949 Lincoln Cent 50% (MS63, $345)
1949 Lincoln Cent 80% (MS65, $489)
1949 Lincoln Cent Double Struck 80% (MS64, $150)
1949-D Lincoln Cent 45% (MS64, $329)
1949-S Lincoln Cent 60% (MS64, $253)
1949-D D/S Jefferson Nickel 75% (AU55, $460)
1949-S Jefferson Nickel 10% (MS66, $647 - $690)

1950

1950-D Lincoln Cent (AU50, $38) (MS62, $51 - $60) (MS63, $29 - $81) (MS64, $51 - $65)
1950-D Lincoln Cent 40% (MS63, $104) (MS64, $141)

1951

1951 Lincoln Cent (MS60, $69) (MS63, $81 - $92)
1951 Lincoln Cent 35% (MS64, $104)
1951-D Lincoln Cent (MS60, $12 - $35) (MS62, $59) (MS63, $21 - $37) (MS64, $31 - $242)
1951-D Lincoln Cent 15% (MS64, $66)
1951 Jefferson Nickel Double Struck 80% (MS63, $147)
1951 Roosevelt Dime 50% (MS62, $322)
1951-S Roosevelt Dime 50% (MS63, $403)
1951-D Franklin Half 20% (AU58, $3,565)

1952

1952 Lincoln Cent (MS62, $59 - $65) (MS63, $59 - $75)
1952 Lincoln Cent 45% (MS63, $89)
1952-D Lincoln Cent (AU58, $15) (MS60, $13 - $18) (MS61, $24 - $51) (MS63, $24 - $45) (MS64, $29 - $48)
1952-D Lincoln Cent 20% (MS65, $92)
1952-D Lincoln Cent 25% (MS64, $112)
1952-D Lincoln Cent 35% (MS64, $104)
1952-D Lincoln Cent 40% (AU58, $94)
1952-D Lincoln Cent 45% (MS63, $100)
1952-D Lincoln Cent 65% (MS64, $103)
1952-D Lincoln Cent Double Struck (MS63, $1,116)
1952-S Lincoln Cent (AU58, $23)
1952-S Lincoln Cent 20% (MS64, $161)
1952-S Lincoln Cent Double Struck (MS63, $374)
1952 Jefferson Nickel Double Struck 50% (MS64, $441)
1952 Jefferson Nickel Double Struck 90% (MS62, $196)
1952 Jefferson Nickel Double Struck 95% (AU58, $299)
1952 Jefferson Nickel Struck on a Dime Planchet (AU55, $432)
1952-S Jefferson Nickel 50% (MS64, $633)
1952-D Franklin Half Struck on a Quarter Planchet (AU58, $1,265)

1953
1953 Lincoln Cent (MS60, $13)
1953 Lincoln Cent 55% (MS64, $161)
1953 Lincoln Cent 60% (MS64, $75)
1953-x Lincoln Cent (MS62, $36)
1953-D Lincoln Cent (MS60, $75) (MS64, $48)
1953-D Lincoln Cent 65% (MS65, $173)
1953-S Jefferson Nickel 5% (MS65, $547)
1953-S Jefferson Nickel 65% (MS66, $559 - $633)
1953-S Washington Quarter Double Stuck 75% (MS63, $1,058)

1954
1954-D Lincoln Cent Double Struck (VF35, $230)
1954-D Jefferson Nickel 70% (MS66, $110)
1954-S Jefferson Nickel 10% (MS61, $253)
1954 Roosevelt Dime (MS62, $69)

1955
1955 Double Struck 70% (MS64, $330)
1955-D Lincoln Cent (MS63, $60)
1955-D Double Struck 80% (MS64, $212)
1955 Jefferson Nickel Struck on a Dime Planchet (AU55, $500 - $1,035)
1955-D Jefferson Nickel 15% (MS66, $403)
1955-S Roosevelt Dime 20% (MS65, $259)
1955 Franklin Half Double Struck 95% (MS64, $1,495 - $1,762)

1956
1956 Lincoln Cent (MS63, $51)
1956-D Lincoln Cent (MS60, $18) (MS62, $33) (MS63, $35 - $59) (MS64, $42 - $253)
1956-x Lincoln Cent (MS63, $37)
1956-x Roosevelt Dime (MS61, $115)

1957
1957 Lincoln Cent (MS63, $37) (MS64, $88)
1957-D Lincoln Cent (MS63, $39 - $54)
1957-D Lincoln Cent 20% (MS64, $218)
1957-D Lincoln Cent 30% (MS62, $69)
1957-D Lincoln Cent 45% (AU58, $150 - $242)
1957-D Lincoln Cent 60% (MS64, $117)
1957-D Lincoln Cent 70% (MS64, $115) (MS65, $127)
1957-D Lincoln Cent 75% (MS63, $115)
1957-D Jefferson Nickel 60% (MS67, $374 - $460)
1957 Mercury Dime (MS60, $54)

1958

1958 Lincoln Cent (MS63, $63)
1958 Lincoln Cent 20% (MS63, $432)
1958-D Lincoln Cent (MS64, $103)
1958-D Lincoln Cent 45% (AG3, $110)
1958-D Lincoln Cent 60% (MS64, $115)
1958-D Lincoln Cent 75% (MS66, $141)
1958-D Lincoln Cent Double Struck 85% (MS63, $184 - $276)
1958-D Jefferson Nickel 65% (MS64, $276) (MS65, $374)
1958-D Jefferson Nickel 65% (MS64, $276)
1958-D Franklin Half Struck on a Quarter Planchet (MS62, $1,380)

1959

1959 Lincoln Cent 85% (MS63, $81)
1959 Lincoln Cent Split Planchet (MS64, $92)
1959-D Lincoln Cent (MS60, $63)
1959-D Jefferson Nickel 75% (MS64, $130)
1959 Washington Quarter 60% (MS63, $2,820)

1960

1960 Lincoln Cent 45% (MS60, $138)
1960-D Lincoln Cent Large Date (MS64, $253)
1960-D Lincoln Cent Large Date Flip Over Double Struck 95% (MS62, $87)
1960 Washington Quarter (MS60, $75)

1961

1961 Lincoln Cent (MS64, $63)
1961 Lincoln Cent 60% (MS62, $75)
1961 Lincoln Cent 80% (MS65, $79)
1961 Lincoln Cent Struck on a Dime Planchet (MS61, $1,175)
1961-D Lincoln Cent (MS63, $73)
1961-D Lincoln Cent 70% (MS65, $84)
1961-D Lincoln Cent 90% (MS64, $94)
1961 Jefferson Nickel 30% (PR66, $3,450 - $4,025)
1961-D Jefferson Nickel 50% (AU58, $345)
1961-D Jefferson Nickel Struck on a Dime Planchet (MS60, $748)

1962

1962 Lincoln Cent (MS64, $44)
1962 Lincoln Cent Ragged Clip (MS65, $31)
1962-D Lincoln Cent 35% (MS63, $156)
1962 Roosevelt Dime 75% (MS64, $138 - $155)

1963

1963-D Lincoln Cent 60% (MS62, $130)
1963 Roosevelt Dime 65% (MS62, $153)
1963 Franklin Half on a Silver Planchet (MS65, $4,994)
1963 Franklin Half Struck on a Nickel Planchet (MS66, $6,900)

1964

1964 Lincoln Cent (AU55, $10) (MS61, $28) (MS64, $132)
1964 Lincoln Cent 40% (MS63, $74)
1964 Lincoln Cent Broadstruck, Brockage (MS65, $81)
1964 Lincoln Cent Double Struck 75% (MS64, $88 - $99)
1964 Lincoln Cent Double Struck 80% (MS64, $74)

Above is a 1964 Triple Struck Lincoln Cent

1964 Lincoln Cent Multiple Strikes (MS65, $1,610)
1964 Lincoln Cent Saddle Struck (MS60, $32) (MS64, $76 - $121)
1964 Lincoln Cent Triple Struck (MS64, $403) (MS65, $550 - $1,150)
1964 Lincoln Cent Triple Struck Saddle Struck (MS64, $805)

1964-D Lincoln Cent (MS60, $17 - $28)
1964-D Lincoln Cent 55% (MS63, $57)
1964-D Lincoln Cent 60% (MS62, $50)
1964-D Lincoln Cent Double Struck (MS60, $44)
1964-D Lincoln Cent Double Struck 90% (MS60, $44)
1964 Jefferson Nickel (MS60, $11)
1964 Jefferson Nickel 7% (MS63, $48)
1964 Jefferson Nickel 5% (MS62, $60)
1964 Jefferson Nickel 40% (AU58, $2,070)
1964 Jefferson Nickel 45% (MS65, $196)
1964 Jefferson Nickel 60% (MS62, $60)
1964 Jefferson Nickel Double Struck (MS63, $207) (MS63, $271)
(MS64, $345)
1964 Jefferson Nickel Struck on a Cent Planchet ($472)
1964 Jefferson Nickel Triple Struck (MS65, $500)
1964-D Jefferson Nickel (MS60, $173)
1964-D Jefferson Nickel 5% (MS62, $192)
1964-D Jefferson Nickel Struck on a Dime Planchet ($748)
1964 Roosevelt Dime (MS63, $57 - $81) (MS60, $87)
1964 Roosevelt Dime 45% (MS62, $165)
1964 Roosevelt Dime 55% (MS63, $188)
1964 Roosevelt Dime 60% (MS64, $150)
1964 Roosevelt Dime 75% (MS61, $4020 (MS63, $161) (MS64,
$130 - $165)
1964 Roosevelt Dime Flip Over Double Stick 50% (MS64,
$1,610)
1964 Roosevelt Dime Triple Struck (MS64, $633)
1964-D Roosevelt Dime (MS60, $161)
1964-D Roosevelt Dime 50% (MS66, $81)
1964-D Roosevelt Dime Double Struck 70% (MS61, $374)
1964-D Roosevelt Dime Struck on a Silver Dime Planchet (MS63,
$1,265)
1964 Washington Quarter (AU55, $150)
1964 Washington Quarter 5% (MS63, $44)
1964-D Washington Quarter Struck on a One Cent Planchet
(MS63, $1,265)
1964 Kennedy Half (MS63, $87 - $173)
1964 Kennedy Half 10% (MS62, $276) (MS64, $64 - $805)
(MS65, $374 - $805)
1964 Kennedy Half 25% (MS64, $822) (MS65, $920)
1964 Kennedy Half 30% (MS64, $920)
1964 Kennedy Half 35% (MS64, $862)
1964 Kennedy Half 50% (MS66, $1,092)
1964-x Kennedy Half 50% (MS65, $460)
1964 Kennedy Half Double Stuck (MS63, $633)

1964 Kennedy Half Struck on a Quarter Planchet (MS63, $750)

1965
1965 Lincoln Cent 5% (MS64, $39)
1965 Lincoln Cent 45% (MS67, $999)
1965 Lincoln Cent Brockage (MS63, $25)
1965 Lincoln Cent Double Struck 60% (MS64, $173 - $179)
1965 Lincoln Cent Double Struck 70% (MS60, $69)
1965 Lincoln Cent Double Struck 75% (MS65, $200) (MS66, $318)
1965 Lincoln Cent Triple Struck (MS64, $978 - $1,616)
1965 Jefferson Nickel 10% (MS64, $69 - $374)
1965 Jefferson Nickel Struck on a Dime Planchet (MS65, $535)
1965 Roosevelt Dime (MS60, $77)
1965 Roosevelt Dime Double Struck 70% (MS61, $377)
1965 Roosevelt Dime Struck on a Silver Planchet (MS60, $1,815)
1965 Washington Quarter 15% (MS63, $14)
1965 Washington Quarter 35% (MS66, $259)
1965 Washington Quarter Struck through Staples (AU50, $1,410)

1966
1966 Lincoln Cent 40% (AU50, $15)
1966 Lincoln Cent 60% (MS64, $633)
1966 Jefferson Nickel 60% (MS66, $550)
1966 Jefferson Nickel Double Struck 40% (MS62, $662)
1966 Jefferson Nickel Double Struck 65% (MS65, $374)
1966 Washington Quarter 45% (MS64, $130)
1966 Washington Quarter on a Roosevelt Planchet 30% (MS64, $470) (MS65, $863)
1966 Washington Quarter Flip Over Double Strike (MS63, $2,760)
1966 Kennedy Half 35% (MS65, $1,840) (MS66, $1,600)
1966 Kennedy Half 50% (MS66, $1,528)
1966 Kennedy Half Struck on Quarter Planchet (MS65, $863)

1967
1967 Lincoln Cent (MS60, $34)
1967 Lincoln Cent 55% (MS62, $47) (MS63, $46)
1967 Lincoln Cent Double Struck 95% (MS60, $47)
1967 Lincoln Cent Struck on a Dime Planchet (F15, $160)
1967 Jefferson Nickel Double Struck (MS64, $318)
1967 Washington Quarter (MS63, $230)
1967 Washington Quarter Struck on a Cent Planchet (MS63, $869 - $1,438

1967 Washington Quarter Struck on a Nickel Planchet (AU50, $184)

1968
1968 Lincoln Cent (MS64, $23)
1968-D Lincoln Cent (AU58, $24)
1968-D Lincoln Cent 15% (MS64, $69)
1968-D Lincoln Cent 60% (MS65, $87)
1968-S Lincoln Cent Double Struck 50% (MS64, $376)
1968-D Jefferson Nickel 68% (MS67, $150)
1968-D Jefferson Nickel Triple Struck (MS64, $1,150)
1968-S Jefferson Nickel (MS63, $57)

1969
1969-D Lincoln Cent (MS60, $28) (MS64, $21- $92)
1969-D Lincoln Cent 30% (AU50, $69)
1969-D Lincoln Cent 55% (MS63, $50)
1969-D Lincoln Cent 60% (MS63, $37)
1969-D Lincoln Cent Double Struck (MS62, $63)
1969-D Lincoln Cent Triple Struck, Saddle Struck (MS65, $587)
1969-S Lincoln Cent 10% with a Straight Clip (MS63, $94)
1969-x Lincoln Cent 75% (MS66, $59)
1969-S Jefferson Nickel Stuck on a Dime Planchet (MS64, $748) (MS65, $1,840)
1969-D Roosevelt Dime (MS65, $432)
1969-D Kennedy Half Dollar Double Struck 40% (MS63, $978)
1969-D Kennedy Half Dollar Double Struck 85% (MS63, $823)
1969-D Kennedy Half Dollar Double Struck 90% (AU58, $1,150)

1970
1970 Lincoln Cent 60% (MS64, $81)
1970-D Lincoln Cent Double Struck 45% (MS62, $84)
1970-D Lincoln Cent Double Struck 75% (MS64, $104)
1970-D Lincoln Cent Double Struck 85% (MS60, $55)
1970-D Lincoln Cent Double Struck (MS63, $207);
1970-D Lincoln Cent Flip Over Triple Saddle Strike (MS62, $1,322)
1970-D Lincoln Cent Saddle Struck (MS66, $550)
1970-S Lincoln Cent Large Date (MS64, $69 - $127)
1970-S Lincoln Cent Large Date 45% (G $44 - $70)
1970-S Lincoln Cent Triple Struck 35% (MS64, $1,035)
1970-x Jefferson Nickel Double Struck (MS63, $134)
1970-D Jefferson Nickel (MS63, $21)
1970-D Jefferson Nickel 55% (MS64, $161)
1970-D Jefferson Nickel 60% (MS63, $23) (MS66, $104)

1970-D Jefferson Nickel 75% (MS62, $177)
1970-D Jefferson Nickel Double Struck (AU58, $253) (MS62, $200) (MS64, $253 - $255)
1970-D Jefferson Nickel Double Struck 45% (AU58, $345) (MS64, $863)
1970-S Jefferson Nickel (MS63, $34)
1970-S Jefferson Nickel 10% (MS62, $21- $92)
1970-S Jefferson Nickel 65% (MS66, $253)
1970 Roosevelt Dime Double Struck 90% (MS62, $26 - $79)
1970-D Roosevelt Dime (MS66, $35)
1970-D Roosevelt Dime Triple Struck, Saddle Struck (MS66, $1,955)
1970-D Washington Quarter 55% (MS64, $127)
1970-D Kennedy Half (MS62, $518)
1970-D Kennedy Half 5% (MS62, $920)
1970-D Kennedy Half 20% (MS63, $823)
1970-S Kennedy Half 10% (PR66, $3,738)

1971

1971-D Lincoln Cent (MS63, $42)
1971-D Lincoln Cent 60% (MS64, $52)
1971-D Lincoln Cent Double Struck 75% (MS60, $36)
1971-D Lincoln Cent Double Struck 85% (MS60, $102)
1971-D Lincoln Cent Double Struck on Dime Planchet (MS62, $863)
1971-D Lincoln Cent Triple Struck 70% (MS62, $259)
1971-S Lincoln Cent 50% (MS65, $104)
1971-S Lincoln Cent 70% (MS66, $150 - $253)
1971-D Jefferson Nickel 15% (AU58, $329)
1971-D Jefferson Nickel 95% (MS64, $98)
1971-D Jefferson Nickel Double Struck (MS64, $299)
1971-D Jefferson Nickel Double Struck 35% (MS62, $412)
1971 Roosevelt Dime (MS60, $25)
1971 Washington Quarter 70% (MS64, $470)
1971-D Washington Quarter (MS63, $219)
1971-D Kennedy Half (MS62, $410)
1971-D Kennedy Half 60% (MS66, $329)
1971-D Kennedy Half 70% (MS64, $353)
1971-D Kennedy Half 80% (MS63, $105)
1971-D Kennedy Half Double Struck 25% (MS62, $1,265)
1971-D Kennedy Half Double Struck 75% (MS62, $518)
1971-D Kennedy Half Double Struck 85% (MS63, $529)
1971-D Eisenhower Dollar 12% (AU58, $253 - $389)

1972

1972 Lincoln Cent (MS65, $31)

1972-D Lincoln Cent (MS62, $24) (MS63, $15 -$21)

1972-D Lincoln Cent 60% (MS64, $27)

1972-D Lincoln Cent Double Struck Flip Over (MS63, $306 - $402)

1972-D Jefferson Nickel (MS60, $17) (MS63, $27) (MS65, $27)

1972-D Jefferson Nickel Double Struck 70% (MS63, $207)

1972-D Jefferson Nickel Struck on a Cent Planchet (VF20, $80)

1972-D Jefferson Nickel Struck on a Nickel Planchet (MS64, $345)

1972-S Jefferson Nickel Double Struck (PR67, $4,315)

1972-D Washington Quarter Struck on a Five Cent Planchet (MS60, $87)

1972-D Roosevelt Dime 70% (MS62, $161)

1972-D Eisenhower Dollar 5% (AU58, $184) (MS64, $196 - $276)

1972-D Eisenhower Dollar 10% (MS60, $180)

1972-D Eisenhower Dollar 35% (MS63, $2,300 - $2,900)

1972-D Eisenhower Dollar Double Struck 10% (MS64, $3,995)

1972-D Eisenhower Dollar Double Struck 25% (MS62, $6,325)

1972-D Eisenhower Dollar Double Struck Broadstruck (PR66, $17,250)

1973

1973 Lincoln Cent Tripe Struck 80%/90% (MS64, $259)

1973-D Lincoln Cent (MS64, $26) (MS65, $29) (MS67, $322)

1973-D Lincoln Cent 50% (MS65, $70)

1973-S Lincoln Cent 60% (MS64, $863)

1973-S Lincoln Cent Double Struck (PR67, $978)

1973 Jefferson Nickel Double Struck 75% (MS60, $60)

1973 Roosevelt Dime 35% (MS62, $92)

1973 Roosevelt Dime Flip Over Triple Strick (G, $1,035)

1973 Washington Quarter (MS63, $12)

1973 Washington Quarter 3% (MS62, $13)

1973 Washington Quarter 50% (AU58, $690)

1973 Washington Quarter Mated Pair (PR65, $4,555) (PR66, $3,760)

1973 Washington Quarter Triple Struck (MS62, $920)

1973-D Kennedy Half (MS62, $230) (MS63, $92)

1973-D Kennedy Half 65% (MS64, $518)

1973-D Kennedy Half Double Struck 40% (MS62, $1,705)

1974

1974 Lincoln Cent Double Struck 55% (MS65, $130)

1974 Lincoln Cent Double Struck 60% (MS60, $118)

1974-D Lincoln Cent (MS63, $24)
1974-S Lincoln Cent 60% (MS65, $138)
1974 Jefferson Nickel 45% (MS66, $190)
1974-D Jefferson Nickel Double Struck 95% (MS60, $40)
1974 Roosevelt Dime Double Struck 90% (MS60, $17)
1974 Washington Quarter 5% (MS64, $18)
1974 Washington Quarter Struck on a Cent (MS63, $604)
1974 Washington Quarter Triple Struck 89% (MS65, $207)
1974-D Washington Quarter Struck on a Cent (MS64, $1,763)
1974 Kennedy Half Double Struck 85% (MS64, $375 - $834)
1974-D Eisenhower Dollar 5% (MS66, $719)
1974-D Eisenhower Dollar Double Struck 90% (MS64, $432 - $460)

1975
1975-D Lincoln Cent (MS64, $39)
1975-D Lincoln Cent 60% (MS60, $34)
1975-D Jefferson Nickel (MS64, $48)
1975-D Jefferson Nickel 5% (MS65, $51)

1976
1976 Lincoln Cent 25% (MS65, $823)
1976 Lincoln Cent Struck on a Dime Planchet 25% (MS65, $1,840)
1976-D Lincoln Cent (MS65, $34)
1976-D Lincoln Cent 80% (MS65, $188)
1976 Jefferson Nickel 15% (MS67, $207)
1976 Jefferson Nickel 25% (MS63, $104 - $765)
1976 Jefferson Nickel 35% (MS64, $104)
1976-D Jefferson Nickel 40% (MS63, $84)
1976-D Jefferson Nickel 50% (MS66, $84)
1976-D Jefferson Nickel 60% (MS66, $67)
1976-D Jefferson Nickel 75% (MS64, $59)
1976 Roosevelt Dime Flip Over Double Struck (MS64, $423)
1976-D Roosevelt Dime Double Struck (AU55, $34)
1976-D Roosevelt Dime Multiple Struck (MS67, $150)
1976 Washington Quarter (MS60, $31 - $55) (MS62, $188) (MS63, $56) (MS65, $57) (MS66, $114)
1976 Washington Quarter 5% (MS66, $92)
1976 Washington Quarter 10% (AU58, $28)
1976 Washington Quarter 15% (MS62, $70) (MS64, $104) (MS65, $109) (MS66, $402)
1976 Washington Quarter 20% (MS65, $153) (MS66, $81)
1976 Washington Quarter 45% (MS64, $356)
1976 Washington Quarter 55% (MS62, $306 - $520)

1976 Washington Quarter 60% (AU58, $805)
1976 Washington Quarter 75% (MS62, $546)
1976 Washington Quarter 85% (MS63, $196) (MS65, $188)
1976 Washington Quarter 90% (MS62, $219)
1976 Washington Quarter Brockage (MS62, $85)
1976 Kennedy Half (MS60, $75 - $165) (MS62, $185) (MS63, $126 - $300) (MS65, $79)
1976 Kennedy Half 5% (AU53, $100) (MS62, $65)
1976 Kennedy Half 10% (AU50, $53) (MS62, $161) (MS65, $188)
1976 Kennedy Half 20% (MS63, $259)
1976 Kennedy Half 50% (MS63, $863)
1976 Kennedy Half 65% (MS65, $647)
1976 Kennedy Half Struck on a Quarter Planchet (MS64, $3,100)
1976-D Kennedy Half (MS63, $120 - $376) (MS66, $161)
1976-D Kennedy Half 40% (MS63, $2,120)
1976-D Kennedy Half 45% (MS64, $2,300)
1976-D Kennedy Half 60% (MS62, $940)
1976-D Kennedy Half 75% (MS64, $495)
1976-D Kennedy Half Double Struck (MS64, $559 - $2,530) (MS66, $633 - $2,250) (MS67, $2,350)
1976 Eisenhower Dollar (MS60, $121) (MS65, $141)
1976 Eisenhower Dollar Type I 95% (MS66, $259)
1976-D Eisenhower Dollar Type I 95% (MS61, $147)
1976-D Eisenhower Dollar Type I Double Struck (MS62, $2,950) (MS63, $353) (MS64, $357)
1976-D Eisenhower Dollar Type II (MS65, $31)
1976-D Eisenhower Dollar Type II 5% (MS65, $110)
1976-D Eisenhower Dollar Type II 90% (MS62, $690)
1976-D Eisenhower Dollar Type II 80% (MS62, $690)
1976-D Eisenhower Dollar Type II 90% (MS62, $705)
1976-D Eisenhower Dollar Type II Double Clipped (MS65, $920)

1977
1977-D Lincoln Cent (MS63, $25)
1977-D Lincoln 15%/25% Three Clips (MS64, $153)
1977 Jefferson Nickel 10% (MS65, $15)
1977 Jefferson Nickel 45% Struck on a Dime Planchet (MS64, $1,840)
1977 Jefferson Nickel Double Struck 90% (MS60, $28 - $105)
1977 Jefferson Nickel Obverse Dent Struck on a Dime Planchet (MS66, $559)
1977-D Jefferson Nickel Struck on A Cent Planchet (XF45, $70)
1977 Roosevelt Dime 10% (MS60, $67)
1977 Roosevelt Dime 60% (MS65, $35)

1977 Washington Quarter (MS63, $57) (MS64, $22) (MS65, $32)
1977-D Kennedy Half Double Struck (AU58, $489)
1977 Eisenhower Dollar 10% (MS60, $345)
1977-D Eisenhower Dollar 17% (MS64, $494)

1978
1978-D Lincoln Cent (MS65, $12)
1978-D Lincoln Cent Double Struck 65% (MS63, $138)
1978 Jefferson Nickel 15% (MS64, $61)
1978 Jefferson Nickel 65% (MS64, $43)
1978 Jefferson Nickel (MS62, $32)
1978 Jefferson Nickel Struck on a Cent Planchet (AU55, $219)
(MS60, $196 -$242)
1978 Roosevelt Dime (MS60, $23) (MS65, $16 - $27)
1978 Roosevelt Dime 20% (MS61, $242)
1978 Washington Quarter (MS64, $32)
1978 Washington Quarter 10% (MS62, $56)
1978 Washington Quarter 15% (MS66, $47)
1978 Washington Quarter 30% (MS63, $57)
1978 Washington Quarter 65% (MS63, $294)
1978 Washington Quarter Double Struck (MS63, $489)
1978 Eisenhower Dollar 5% (MS64, $153 - $184) (MS65, $46)
1978 Eisenhower Dollar 10% (MS60, $126) (MS64, $322)
1978 Eisenhower Dollar 15% (MS63, $633)
1978 Eisenhower Dollar 30% (MS66, $1,958- $2,070)
1978 Eisenhower Dollar 35% (MS64, $2,360) (MS65, $2,070)
1978 Eisenhower Dollar 40% (MS64, $2,530)
1978 Eisenhower Dollar 45% (MS65, $2,875)
1978-D Eisenhower Dollar 5% (MS62, $253) (MS64, $212)
(MS65, $115 - $276) (MS66, $259)
1978-D Eisenhower Dollar 10% (MS64, $259)

1979
1979-D Lincoln Cent (MS64, $15)
1979-D Lincoln Cent Triple Curved Planchet (MS64, $130)
1979 Jefferson Nickel 35% (MS60, $130)
1979 Jefferson Nickel 45% (MS65, $30)
1979 Jefferson Nickel 60% (MS65, $30)
1979 Jefferson Nickel 5% Struck on a Cent Planchet (MS65,
$978 - $1,500)
1979-D Jefferson Nickel Double Struck 65% (MS65, $805)
1979-D Roosevelt Dime 70% (MS63, $92)
1979-D Roosevelt Dime Triple Struck Flip-over (MS64, $1495)
1979 Washington Quarter (MS63, $21)

133

1979 Washington Quarter 20 % w/Curved Clip (MS64, $177 - $200)
1979 Washington Quarter Triple Struck 40% (MS66, $412 - $750)
1979 Kennedy Half (MS60, $45 - $63) (MS64, $188)
1979 Kennedy Half 5% (AU58, $101)
1979 Kennedy Half 10% (MS61, $69 - $276) (MS62, $94) (MS64, $105)
1979 Kennedy Half 15% (MS61, $150)
1979 Kennedy Half Broadstruck (MS65, $133)
1979 Kennedy Half Struck on a Susan B (MS64, $978)
1979-P Susan B Broadstruck (MS63, $30)
1979-P Susan B (MS60, $76 - $151) (MS63, $106 - $141) (MS64, $230) (MS65, $115)
1979-P Susan B 10% (MS63, $46) (MS65, $259) (MS66, $276)
1979-P Susan B 15% (MS64, $92 - $155)
1979-P Susan B 20% (MS64, $122 - $253)
1979-P Susan B Struck on a Quarter Planchet (AU58, $431) (MS61, $690)
1979-D Susan B 55% (MS66, $440)
1979-D Susan B Mated Pair (MS64, $1,645)

1980
1980 Lincoln Cent Double Struck (MS65, $52)
1980 Lincoln Cent Double Struck 85% (MS65, $183 - $188)
1980-D Lincoln Cent (AU55, $11) (MS64, $14)
1980-D Lincoln Cent 55% (MS65, $59)
1980-D Lincoln Cent Struck on Scrap (MS65, $173)
1980-D Lincoln Cent Triple Struck (MS62, $345)
1980-P Jefferson Nickel (MS60, $24) (MS64, $45)
1980-P Jefferson Nickel 50% (MS64, $138)
1980-P Jefferson Nickel 55% (MS64, $47 - $89)
1980-P Jefferson Nickel Double Struck 55% (MS64, $460)
1980-P Jefferson Nickel Double Struck 85% (MS60, $21 - $188) (MS65, $46)
1980-P Jefferson Nickel Obverse Brockage (MS63, $99)
1980-P Jefferson Nickel Struck on a Cent Planchet 10% (MS63, $895)
1980-P Jefferson Nickel Struck on a Cent Planchet 20% (MS63, $690 - $1,840) (MS64, $1,265)
1980-P Jefferson Nickel Struck on a Cent Planchet 25% (MS65, $1,006)
1980-P Jefferson Nickel Struck on a Cent Planchet 30% (MS64, $882 - $2,750)

1980-P Jefferson Nickel Struck on a Cent Planchet (MS63, $357-$415) (MS64, $259)
1980-P Jefferson Nickel Triple Struck (MS63, $520)
1980-D Jefferson Nickel 20% (MS64, $1,265)
1980-D Jefferson Nickel 50% (MS67, $1,495)
1980-D Jefferson Nickel Double Clip 25% (MS67, $127)
1980-D Jefferson Nickel Double Struck 75% (MS62, $81)
1980-D Jefferson Nickel Double Struck 80% (MS63, $42)
1980-P Washington Quarter (AU50, $11) (MS63, $12)
1980-D Washington Quarter Double Struck 85% (MS60, $26)
1980-P Kennedy Half 15% (MS60, $153)
1980-P Kennedy Half Struck on a Susan B (MS62, $1,650)
1980-S Susan B 45% (MS64, $882)

1981
1981 Lincoln Cent 45% (MS60, $23)
1981 Lincoln Cent Double Struck Flip Over (MS64, $125)
1981 Lincoln Cent Struck on a Dime Planchet (MS65, $520)
1981 Lincoln Cent Triple Struck 50%/70% (MS64, $1,035)
1981-D Lincoln Cent (MS63, $42) (MS64, $23)
1981-D Lincoln Cent Struck on a Dime Planchet (MS60, $605)
1981-P Jefferson Nickel 50% (MS64, $138)
1981-P Jefferson Nickel Bonded Pair (MS65, $1,610)
1981-P Jefferson Nickel Double Struck 80% (MS60, $98)
1981-P Jefferson Nickel Double Struck 85% (MS60, $18 - $165)
1981-P Jefferson Nickel Struck on a Cent Planchet (MS64, $1,095)
1981-D Jefferson Nickel Double Struck 85% (MS60, $18)
1981-P Roosevelt Dime Double Struck 80% (MS60, $36)
1981-P Washington Quarter 15% (MS60, $120) (MS64, $30)
1981-P Kennedy Half (MS60, $127 - $140) (MS62, $200 - $265)

1982
1982 Lincoln Cent Broadstruck, Brockage (MS65, $80)
1982 Lincoln Cent Bronze Plated LD (MS63, $35)
1982 Lincoln Cent Bronze Triple Struck Saddle Struck (MS65, $235)
1982 Lincoln Cent LD Struck on a Dime Planchet (MS63, $185)
1982 Lincoln Cent SD Struck on a Dime Planchet (MS64, $253 - $435)
1982 Lincoln Cent Zinc LD Double Struck (MS64, $100) (MS65, $70)
1982-D Lincoln Cent Zinc LD (MS65, $35)
1982-P Jefferson Nickel Double Struck 95% (MS64, $40)
1982-P Jefferson Nickel Triple Struck (MS64, $635)

1982-D Jefferson Nickel Double Struck 75% (MS60, $36 - $75)

1983
1983 Lincoln Cent (MS60, $1.20 - $30)
1983 Lincoln Cent 60% (MS65, $30 - $35)
1983 Lincoln Cent Broadstruck (MS63, $28)
1983 Lincoln Cent Brockage (MS60, $22)
1983 Lincoln Cent Double Struck 75% (MS60, $40) (MS64, $376)
1882-P Jefferson Nickle Broadstruck, Brockage (AU55, $14)
1983-P Jefferson Nickel Double Struck 5% (MS64, $36)
1983-P Jefferson Nickel Double Struck 50% (MS64, $127)
1983-P Jefferson Nickel Double Struck 75% (MS60, $46)
1983-P Jefferson Nickel Double Struck 80% (MS61, $48) (MS64, $36) (MS65, $36)
1983-P Jefferson Nickel Double Struck 85% (MS63, $105) (MS64, $23 - $55) (MS65, $48)
1983-P Jefferson Nickel Double Struck 90% (MS60, $25 - $35) (MS62, $35) (MS63, $38) (MS64, $36 - $42) (MS65, $46 - $50)
1983-P Jefferson Nickel Double Struck 95% (MS60, $21 - $25) (MS65, $25 - $40)
1983-P Jefferson Nickel Triple Struck 70% (AU58, $282)
1983-D Jefferson Nickel 50% (MS66, $161)
1983-P Roosevelt Dime 75% (MS60, $34)
1983-D Roosevelt Dime MS61, $17)
1983-P Washington Quarter (MS60, $32 - $179) (MS62, $28) (MS63, $23- $40) (MS64, $29 - $45) (MS65, $18 - $40)
1983-P Washington Quarter 5% (MS64, $45)
1983-P Washington Quarter 10% (MS60, $18) (MS64, $3.50 - $106) (MS65, $94)
1983-P Washington Quarter 15% (MS60, $35 - $48) (MS63, $34) (MS64, $40 - $112)
1983-P Washington Quarter 20% (MS62, $38 - $45)
1983-P Washington Quarter 25% (MS65, $153) (MS66, $195)
1983-P Washington Quarter 30% - 90% (AU58, $105) (MS60, $36 -$50) (MS60, $153) (MS62, $106) (MS64, $188 - $235)
1983-P Washington Quarter Double Struck (MS64, $36)
1983-P Washington Quarter Double Struck 20% (MS62, $47)
1983-P Washington Quarter Double Struck 30% (MS60, $130)
1983-P Washington Quarter Double Struck 55% (AU58, $425) (MS64, $130)
1983-P Kennedy Half (AU55, $121) (MS62, $48 - $127)
1983-P Kennedy Half 10%-15% (MS64, $121) (MS65, $142 - $147)
1983-P Kennedy Half 65% (MS65, $489)
1983-P Kennedy Half 70% (MS65, $633)

1984
1984 Lincoln Cent (MS65, $20)
1984 Lincoln Cent 75% (MS63, $28)
1984-D Lincoln Cent Double Struck 85% (MS64, $141)
1984-P Jefferson Nickel (MS62, $21)
1984-P Jefferson Nickel Broadstruck on a Dime Planchet (MS67, $588 - $1064)
1984-P Jefferson Nickel Double Struck (MS62, $87) (MS64, $80) (MS65, $322)
1984-P Jefferson Nickel Double Struck 75% (MS60, $36)
1984-P Jefferson Nickel Double Struck on a Dime Planchet (MS64, $1,495)
1984-P Washington (MS64, $63)
1984-P Washington Quarter 10% -15% (MS63, $42- $50) (MS66, $84)
1984-P Washington Quarter 50% (MS60, $70)
1984-P Kennedy Half (MS63, $45 - $55)

1985
1985 Lincoln Cent (MS64, $17)
1985 Lincoln Cent Double Struck (AU50, $28)
1985 Lincoln Cent Double Struck 70% (MS64, $65)
1985 Lincoln Cent Double Struck 75% (MS64, $95)
1985-P Jefferson Nickel 90% (MS60, $19)
1985-P Jefferson Nickel Clip (MS63, $66)
1985-P Jefferson Nickel Double Struck (AU55, $54) (MS62, $94)
1985-P Jefferson Nickel Double Struck 45% (MS64, $115)
1985-D Jefferson Nickel (MS60, $27)
1985-D Jefferson Nickel 50% (MS66, $161)
1985-P Roosevelt Dime Double Struck 75% (MS66, $177)
1985-P Washington Quarter (MS64, $18)
1985-P Washington Quarter Double Struck 60% - 65% (MS62, $200 - $260) (MS63, $329)
1985-P Washington Quarter Multiple Struck (MS66, $805)
1985-P Washington Quarter Mated Pair (MS65, $1,725)
1985-P Washington Quarter Triple Struck (MS65, $765)

1986
1986 Lincoln Cent (MS64, $13 - $20)
1986-D Jefferson Nickel (MS62, $54)
1986-D Jefferson Nickel D over S 70% (AU55, $253)
1986-P Roosevelt Dime Double Struck 70% (MS62, $84)
1986-P Washington Quarter (AU55, $28 - $35) (MS64, $27)

137

1987

1987 Lincoln Cent Double Struck 75% (MS63, $115) (MS64, $74)
1987-D Lincoln Cent (MS64, $18)
1987-P Jefferson Nickel 35% (MS64, $138)
1987-D Jefferson Nickel (MS63, $35)
1987-D Washington Quarter (MS65, $44)
1987-D Washington Quarter Triple Struck Clipped Planchet (AU53, $165)

1988

1988 Lincoln Cent 10% (MS64, $92)
1988 Lincoln Cent Brockage, Broadstruck (MS63, $24)
1988 Lincoln Cent Flip Over Double Struck (MS63, $110) (MS65, $147)
1988-D Lincoln Cent (MS64, $12 - $30)
1988-P Jefferson Nickel Ragged Clip (AU58, $185)
1988-D Jefferson Nickel Multi-Struck 60% (MS67, $104)
1988-P Roosevelt Dime Double Struck 65% - 95% (MS63, $130 - $376)
1988-D Roosevelt Dime (MS63, $29)
1988-P Washington Quarter (MS63, $69)
1988-P Kennedy Half 5% (MS66, $50)

1989

1989 Lincoln Cent 15% (MS67, $1,095)
1989 Lincoln Cent 45% (MS60, $24)
1989 Lincoln Cent Broadstruck, Brockage (AU55, $14)
1989 Lincoln Cent Double Struck 65% (MS66, $70)
1989-D Lincoln Cent (MS65, $23)
1989-D Lincoln Cent 65% (MS64, $40)
1989-P Jefferson Nickel 45% -55% (MS60, $47) (MS62, $26 - $40)
1989-P Jefferson Nickel Double Struck (MS63, $79)
1989-P Jefferson Nickel Triple Struck (MS64, $403)
1989-P Roosevelt Dime 70% (MS63, $74) (MS65, $45)
1989-D Roosevelt Dime (MS64, $29)
1989-P Washington Quarter 10% (MS64, $115) (MS65, $38)
1989-P Washington Quarter 20% (MS66, $329)
1989-P Kennedy Half (MS61, $51) (MS63, $69 - $99) (MS66, $110)
1989-P Kennedy Half Double Struck 60% (MS64, $1,620)
1989-P Kennedy Half Double Struck 65% (MS62, $823)

1990

1990 Lincoln Cent 5% (MS64, $30)

1990 Lincoln Cent 15% (MS64, $35)
1990 Lincoln Cent 35% (MS63, $36) (MS64, $40)
1990 Lincoln Cent 40% (MS64, $30- $40)
1990 Lincoln Cent 45% (MS63, $23)
1990 Lincoln Cent 50% (MS65, $56)
1990-D Lincoln Cent (MS63, $10)
1990-P Jefferson Nickel Double Struck with Brockage (MS64, $220)
1990-P Roosevelt Dime 30% (MS62, $69)
1990-P Washington Quarter 50% (MS66, $56)
1990-P Kennedy Half (MS60, $127) (MS62, $66) (MS63, $87 - $138) (MS64, $44 - $277) (MS65, $87) (MS66, $84)
1990-P Kennedy Half 5% (MS65, $99)
1990-P Kennedy Half 10% (MS62, $84) (MS63, $104) (MS65, $106 - $115)
1990-P Kennedy Half 15% (MS65, $173) (MS66, $153 - $255)
1990-P Kennedy Half 20% (MS66, $276)
1990-D Kennedy Half 15% (MS64, $150)

1991
1991 Lincoln Cent 35% (MS62, $26 - $47)
1991-D Lincoln Cent (MS64, $23)
1991-D Lincoln Cent Double Struck 70% (MS63, $79)
1991-P Roosevelt Dime (MS62, $23)
1991-P Roosevelt Dime 30% - 35% (MS63, $30) (MS65, $94)
1991-D Kennedy Half 50% (MS62, $547)

1992
1992 Lincoln Cent Double Struck 75% (MS60, $34) (MS63, $67)

1993
1993 Lincoln Cent Broadstruck, Double Struck (MS60, $24) (MS63, $22 - $44) (MS64, $19 - $56) (MS65, $40)
1993 Lincoln Cent Double Struck (MS65, $58)
1993 Lincoln Cent Double Struck 80% (MS60, $58)
1993 Lincoln Cent Struck on a Dime Planchet (MS65, $173)
1993-D Lincoln Cent (MS64, $19)
1993-P Jefferson Nickel Double Struck 45% (MS65, $84)
1993-P Jefferson Nickel Double Struck 75% (MS61, $59 -$74)
1993-D Jefferson Nickel (MS63, $11)
1993-P Roosevelt Dime Brockage (MS63, $16)
1993-P Washington Quarter Double Struck 10% (AU58, $432)
1993-P Washington Quarter Double Struck 55% - 60% (MS64, $282 - $306)

1993-P Washington Quarter Triple Struck 65% (MS66, $382)

1994

1994 Lincoln Cent Broadstruck, Brockage (MS63, $18)
1994 Lincoln Cent Double Struck 70% (MS62, $184)
1994-D Lincoln Cent (MS64, $11 - $20)
1994-P Jefferson Nickel (MS64, $38)
1994-P Jefferson Nickel 12% (MS64, $23)
1994-P Jefferson Nickel 25% (MS65, $49)
1994-D Roosevelt Dime 90% (MS65, $6)
1994-P Roosevelt Dime 75% (MS65, $6)
1994-P Roosevelt Dime Double Struck (MS63, $41)
1994-P Washington Quarter 10% (MS62, $32)
1994-D Washington Quarter (AU58, $26) (MS62, $34 - $127)

1995

1995 Lincoln Cent Counterbrockage, Flipover, Double Strike (MS63, $18)
1995 Lincoln Cent Double Struck (MS64, $10) (MS65, $40)
1995 Lincoln Cent Double Struck 70% (MS65, $97)
1995 Lincoln Cent Double Struck 75% (MS60, $85)
1995 Lincoln Cent Triple Stuck 75%/85% (MS64, $165)
1995-D Lincoln Cent (MS65, $13)
1995-P Jefferson Nickel 25% (MS60, $39)
1995-P Jefferson Nickel 40% (MS60, $85)
1995-P Jefferson Nickel 50% (MS64, $65)
1995-P Jefferson Nickel Brockage 10% (MS64, $18)
1995-P Jefferson Nickel Double Struck (MS60, $60) (MS63, $50) (MS64, $105) (MS65, $20) (MS66, $750)
1995-P Roosevelt Dime 20% (MS64, $36 - $55)
1995-D Roosevelt Dime (MS65, $75)
1995-D Roosevelt Dime 45% (MS66, $60)
1995-P Washington Quarter (MS63, $30 - $45) (MS65, $60 - $70)
1995-P Washington Quarter 55% (MS64, $90)
1995-P Washington Quarter Brockage (MS64, $85)
1995-P Washington Quarter Double Struck (MS65, $220) (MS66, $175)
1995-D Washington Quarter (MS63, $30 - $45) (MS64, $40) (MS65, $19 - $36)
1995-D Washington Quarter 45% (MS65, $65) (MS66, $375)
1995-P Kennedy Half 10% (MS64, $95)

1996

1996 Lincoln Cent (MS64, $30) (MS65, $20)

1996 Lincoln Cent 40% (MS65, $38 - $55)
1996 Lincoln Cent Die Cap (MS63, $115)
1996 Lincoln Cent Double Struck 25% (MS66, $400)
1996 Lincoln Cent Double Struck Brockage 45% (MS64, $200)
1996 Lincoln Cent Double Struck 65% - 80% (MS61, $74 - $95)
(MS65, $55)
1996 Lincoln Cent Triple Struck (MS68, $550)
1996-D Lincoln Cent (MS66, $20)
1996-D Lincoln Cent 75% Triple Struck (MS62, $120 - $155)
1996-P Jefferson Nickel (MS64, $30)
1996-P Jefferson Nickel 50% - 55% (MS60, $23) (MS64, $60)
(MS65, $40)
1996-P Jefferson Nickel 65% - 85% (MS60, $45) (MS61, $26)
(MS64, $35 - $230) (MS65, $40 - $130)
1996-P Jefferson Nickel Double Struck (MS63, $285)
1996-P Jefferson Nickel Triple Struck (MS64, $230)
1996-D Jefferson Nickel Double Struck (MS65, $105)
1996-D Jefferson Nickel Saddle Struck (MS64, $46)
1996-P Roosevelt Dime (MS63, $11)
1996-P Roosevelt Dime 25% - %35 (MS60, $48) (MS65, $65)
1996-P Roosevelt Dime Broadstruck, Brockage (MS66, $35)
1996-P Roosevelt Dime Curved Clip 10% (MS64, $110)
1996-P Roosevelt Dime Double Struck (AU58, $2,100)
1996-P Washington Quarter 30% (MS65, $165)
1996-P Washington Quarter Double Struck (MS65, $82)
1996-D Washington Quarter 15% (MS64, $175)
1996-D Washington Quarter Double Struck 80% (MS65, $82)
1996-D Washington Quarter Triple Clip (MS62, $105)

1997
1997 Lincoln Cent 25% (MS64, $56)
1997 Lincoln Cent 60% (MS60, $34)
1997 Lincoln Cent 75% (MS65, $60)
1997 Double Struck, Broadstruck (MS66, $51 - $375)
1997 Double Struck 15% (MS68, $260)
1997 Double Struck 75% (MS65, $60)
1997-D Lincoln Cent (MS66, $31)
1997-D Kennedy Half 45% (MS64, $475 - $632)
1997-D Kennedy Half 50% (AU50, $547)
1997-D Kennedy Half 70% (MS64, $920) (MS65, $490)

1998
1998 Lincoln Cent (MS63, $12) (MS65, $18) (MS66, $25)
1998 Lincoln Cent 25% (MS66, $55)
1998 Lincoln Cent Brockage (MS65, $31)

1998 Lincoln Cent Broadstruck, Brockage (MS61, $35) (MS64, $35 - $82) (MS65, $31)
1998 Lincoln Cent Double Struck (MS65, $235) (MS66, $90 - $105)
1998 Lincoln Cent Double Struck 30% - 90% (MS62, $60 - $90) (MS64, $40 - $415) (MS65, $55 - $155) (MS66, $104)
1998 Lincoln Cent Double Struck w/Die Cap (MS67, $950)
1998 Lincoln Cent Mated Pair (MS65, $175)
1998 Lincoln Cent Saddle Struck (MS65, $235)
1998 Lincoln Cent Triple Struck (MS62, $105) (MS64, $70 - $90)
1998-D Lincoln Cent (MS63, $23 - $25) (MS64, $14)
1998-D Lincoln Cent 25% (MS62, $35) (MS64, $35) (MS65, $55) (MS66, $31)
1998-D Lincoln Cent Double Struck 70% (MS63, $37)
1998-P Jefferson Nickel (MS64, $12)
1998-P Jefferson Nickel Double Struck (MS63, $325)
1998-P Jefferson Nickel Double Struck Flip Over (MS64, $605)
1998-P Jefferson Nickel Multiple Struck (MS63, $550)
1998-P Jefferson Nickel Triple Struck (MS60, $253) (MS64, $1,645)
1998-P Roosevelt Dime 10% (MS66, $18)
1998-P Roosevelt Dime Brockage (MS62, $24)
1998-P Washington Quarter (MS62, $35) (MS64, $90 - $160) (MS65, $21)
1998-P Washington Quarter 5% (MS63, $35) (MS64, $40)
1998-P Washington Quarter 25% - 50% (MS64, $75 - $140)
1998-P Washington Quarter Double Struck (MS65, $80 - $180)
1998-P Washington Quarter Triple Struck (MS63, $375 - $1,265) (MS65, $700)
1998-D Washington Quarter 10% (AU58, $175)
1998-P Kennedy Half 5% (MS66, $56)

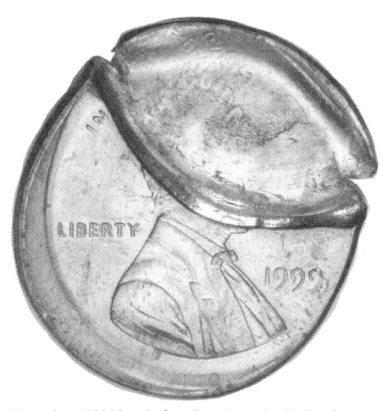

Above is a 1999 Lincoln Cent Broadstruck with Brockage

1999
1999 Lincoln Cent (MS63, $10 - $70) (MS64, $10 - $275) (MS65, $10 - $40) (MS66, $12 - $110) (MS67, $140)
1999 Lincoln Cent 20 % - 25% (MS64, $22 - $25) (MS65, $25 - $75)
1999 Lincoln Cent Broadstruck and Brockage (MS61, $35) (MS66, $30 - $85)
1999 Lincoln Cent Double Struck (MS63, $145) (MS64, $225) (MS65, $75 - $1,125) (MS66, $72)
1999 Lincoln Cent Double Struck Broadstruck (MS65, $30 - $90)
1999 Lincoln Cent Double Struck Die Cap (MS66, $489)
1999 Lincoln Cent Double Struck Flip Over (MS66, $215)
1999 Lincoln Cent Double Struck, Rotated (MS65, $230)
1999 Lincoln Cent Mated Pair (MS64, $175)

1999 Lincoln Cent Obverse. Cap, Bonded, Double Struck (MS64, $184 - $605)
1999 Lincoln Cent Quadruple Struck (MS65, $360)
1999-D Lincoln Cent (MS65, $15) (MS66, $15)
1999-D D over S Doubled Die (MS66, $375)
1999-P Jefferson Nickel (MS65, $15 - $130) (MS66, $16 - $62)
1999-P Brockage (MS64, $22 - $85)
1999-P Jefferson Nickel Double Struck (MS64, $185 - $215)
1999-D Jefferson Nickel (MS62, $18) (MS63, $36) (MS65, $20 - $25)
1999-D Jefferson Nickel 40% - 75% (MS63, $26 - $35) (MS64, $20 - $120) (MS65, $20 - $36 - $50) (MS66, $40 - $80) (MS67, $110)
1999-D Jefferson Nickel Double Struck 70% - 98% (AU58, $25) (MS 61, $55) (MS63, $45 - $150) (MS64, $21 - $110) (MS65, $85)
1999-P Roosevelt Dime (MS62, $30) (MS63, $15 - $20) (MS64, $15 - $30) (MS65, $16 - $25)
1999-P Roosevelt Dime 20% - 25% (MS64, $16) (MS66, $20)
1999-P Roosevelt Dime 55% (MS66, $65)
1999-P Roosevelt Dime Brockage (MS66, $35)
1999-P Roosevelt Dime Broadstruck (MS66, $50)
1999-P Roosevelt Dime Double Struck (MS66, $485) (MS67, $920)
1999-D Roosevelt Dime Double Struck (MS64, $60)
1999-P Quarter Die Cap Double Struck (MS65, $1,265)
1999-P Connecticut Quarter 5% - 20% (MS62, $40 - $45) (MS65, $87) (MS67, $276)
1999-P Connecticut Quarter 35% (MS63, $720) (MS66, $250 - $690)
1999-P Connecticut Quarter Double Stuck (MS64, $104 - $445) (MS65, $978) (MS67, $805)
1999-P Connecticut Quarter Struck on SBA (MS63, $2,450)
1999-P Connecticut Quarter Triple Struck (MS64, $445)
1999-P Connecticut Quarter Quadruple Struck (MS65, $490 - $575)
1999-D Connecticut Quarter (XF45, $115) (AU53, $25 - $30) (MS64, $50 - $55) (MS65, $35 - $60) (MS66, $25)
1999-x Connecticut Quarter Fold Over Strike (MS65, $4,889)
1999-P Delaware Quarter (MS60, $125) (MS64, $80)
1999-P Delaware Quarter 30% (MS64, $230) (MS65, $345)
1999-P Delaware Quarter Double Struck 30% (MS66, $490 - $865)

1999-P Delaware Quarter on Scrap Planchet 20% (MS64, $400)
1999-D Delaware Quarter (MS63, $160 - $170) (MS64, $190)
(MS65, $145 - $177)
1999-D Delaware Quarter 65% - 75% (MS63, $210) (MS64,
$220 - $230)
1999-D Delaware Quarter Struck on a Nickel Planchet (AU58,
$1,035) (MS62, $360) (MS64, $1,410)
1999-P Georgia Quarter (MS63, $76 - $325) (MS64, $127)
(MS65, $84 - $155) (MS67, $127)
1999-P Georgia Quarter Double Struck (MS62, $305) (MS63,
$325) (MS64, $105)
1999-P Georgia Quadruple Struck (MS65, $588)
1999-P Georgia Triple Struck (MS63, $450) (MS64, $495)
1999-D Georgia Quarter (AU55, $50) (MS60, $55) (MS63, $173)
(MS64, $55) (MS65, $35 - $60)
1999-D Georgia Quarter Broadstruck (XF45, $25) (MS63, $15 -
$50) (MS64, $50) (MS66, $25)
1999-x Georgia Quarter 75% (MS67, $230)
1999-x Georgia Quarter Triple Struck ($415)
1999-P New Jersey Double Struck 40% - 75% (MS63, $210)
(MS66, $490 - $720)
1999-x New Jersey 50% - 65% (MS62, $270) (MS64, $190)
(MS65, $196)
1999-D New Jersey (MS64, $110 - $280)
1999-P Pennsylvania Quarter (MS60, $55) (MS64, $150) (MS65,
$130 - $345)
1999-P Pennsylvania Quarter 35% (MS67, $865)
1999-P Pennsylvania Quarter Double Struck (MS67, $635)
1999-D Pennsylvania Quarter (AU50, $90)
1999-D Pennsylvania Quarter 10% w/Clip (AU58, $275)
1999-D Pennsylvania Quarter 75% (MS65, $345)
1999-D Pennsylvania Quarter Multiple Struck (MS64, $690)
1999-x Pennsylvania Quarter 50% - 55% (MS64, $220) (MS65,
$215)
1999-D Kennedy Half (MS60, $144)
1999-P Susan B. (MS64, $70 -$330) (MS65, $260) (MS66, $235
- $855) (MS67, $196) (MS68, $225 - $885) (PS65, $403)
1999-P Susan B. Broadstruck (MS65, $150) (MS67, $175 -
$450)
1999-P Susan B. Double Struck (AU58, $500) (MS62, (MS63,
$404 - $460) (MS64, $1,265) (MS65, $605 - $1,955) (MS66,
$750 - $1,865)

1999-P Susan B. Flip Over Double Struck (MS64, $2,450) (MS65, $1,150)
1999-P Susan B. (MS64, $3,450)
1999-P Susan B. Triple Struck (MS65, $605 - $4,600)
1999-P Susan B. Struck on a Quarter Planchet (MS64, $2,185) (MS66, $920)
1999-P Susan B. Struck on Georgia Quarter (MS64, $6,325)

2000

2000 Lincoln Cent (MS63, $10) (MS64, $$805) 14) (MS65, $16 - $33) (MS66, $62)
2000 Lincoln Cent 50% (MS63, $42) (MS64, $40)
2000 Lincoln Cent Broad Struck (MS64, $46 - $52) (MS65, $46) (MS66, $115)
2000 Lincoln Cent Broad Struck, Brockage (MS64, $20 - $85) (MS65, $36) (MS67, $75)
2000 Lincoln Cent Brockage (MS64, $38 - $40)
2000 Lincoln Cent Double Struck (MS60, $28) (MS64, $38) (MS65, $64 - $70)
2000 Lincoln Cent Double Struck 15% - 80% (MS63, $56 - $83) (MS64, $153 - $196)
2000 Lincoln Cent Double Struck Flip Over 10% - 85% (MS63, $90 - $230) (MS65, $96) (MS66, $90)
2000 Lincoln Cent Saddle Struck (MS64, $88)
2000 Lincoln Cent Struck on a Dime Planchet (MS63, $300)
2000 Lincoln Cent Triple Struck (MS66, $230 - $380)
2000-D Lincoln Cent Double Struck (AU58, $55) (MS64, $56 - $118)
2000-D Jefferson Nickel (MS64, $36 - $47) (MS65, $21 - $22)
2000-D Jefferson Nickel 45% - 85% (MS63, $56) (MS64, $45 - $95) (MS65, $20 - $36) (MS66, $26 - $46) (MS67, $138)
2000-P Roosevelt Dime (MS63, $45) (MS64, $64) (MS65, $16 - $66)
2000-P Roosevelt Dime Double Struck (MS64, $26)
2000-P Massachusetts Quarter (MS64, $185) (MS66, $60 - $177)
2000-P Massachusetts Quarter Partial Collar (MS65, $16 - $45)
2000-P Massachusetts Quarter Quadruple Struck (MS65, $600 - $605)
2000-P Maryland Quarter (MS64, $39) (MS64, $75) (MS67, $260)
2000-P Maryland Quarter Triple Struck (MS62, $360)

146

2000-P New Hampshire Quarter (MS63, $92) (MS64, $20 - $220) (MS65, $30 - $230) (MS66, $30 -$255) (MS67, $84 - $215) (MS68, $245 - $260)

2000-P New Hampshire Quarter Broadstruck (MS64, $20 - $25) (MS67, $85)

2000-P New Hampshire Quarter Broadstruck, Brockage (MS66, $85)

2000-P New Hampshire Quarter Double Struck (MS64, $355) (MS66, $380 - $530)

2000-P South Carolina Quarter (MS63, $20 - $40) (MS64, $47 - $255) (MS66, $127) (MS67, $70 - $145) (MS68, $205 - $435)

2000-P South Carolina Quarter Double Stuck (MS66, $633)

2000-P South Carolina Quarter Triple Struck (MS64, $380)

2000-P Virginia Quarter (MS63, $19) (MS66, $26 - $255)

2000-P Virginia Quarter Double Struck (MS63, $435)

2000-P Virginia Quarter Triple Struck (MS64, $555)

2000-D Virginia Quarter Struck 7 times (MS64, 720)

2000-P Sacagawea Double Struck (MS65, $1,060 - $1,800) (MS66, ($980)

2000-P Sacagawea Mule with Washington Quarter (MS66, $31,000)

2000-P Sacagawea Quadruple Struck (MS63, $1,265) (MS64, $2,750 - $4,900) (MS67, $1,725 - $2,650)

2000-P Sacagawea Struck Six times (MS65, $3,000)

2000-P Sacagawea Triple Struck (MS64, $2,175) (MS65, $2,070)

2001

2001 Lincoln Cent Clashed Dies (MS64, $56) (MS65, $11) (MS66, $45)

2001 Lincoln Cent Broadstruck, Brockage (MS63, $26) (MS64, $29) (MS65, $75)

2001 Lincoln Cent Double Struck (MS64, $20) (MS65, $156) (MS66, $75 - $235)

2001 Lincoln Cent Double Struck NS Indent (MS65, $156)

2001-D Lincoln Cent Triple Struck (MS67, $165)

2001-P Roosevelt Dime Brockage, Clashed Dies (MS64, $79)

2001-P Roosevelt Dime Mated Pair (MS65, $890)

2001-P North Carolina (MS62, $105) (MS63, $36) (MS65, $34 - $150)

2001-P North Carolina Double Struck (MS65, $470)

2001-P North Carolina Quadruple Struck (MS63, $560 - $610) (MS64, $695)

2001-P North Carolina Triple Struck (MS66, $500)
2001-P New York Double Struck (MS62, $480) (MS64, $470)
(MS65, $500 - $530) (MS66, $500)
2001-P New York Triple Struck (MS64, $550) (MS65, $700)

2002

2003
2003-D Lincoln Cent Double Struck (MS64, $150 - $460)

2004

2005
2005-P Jefferson Nickel (MS63, $127)

2006
2006-P Jefferson Nickel (MS66FS, $435)

2007
2007-P Roosevelt Dime (MS63, $55)
2007-S Thomas Jefferson $1 Double Struck (PR69, $650)
2007-D Idaho Double Struck (MS66, $9400
2007 Madison $1 Missing Letter Edge (MS64, $405)

2008

2009

2010

2011

2012

2013

2014

2015

2016

2017

2018

2019

2020

2021

Chapter 15 – Modern Day Coin Errors

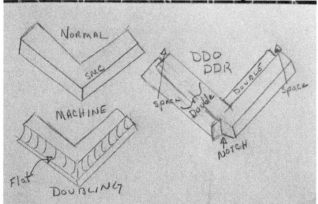

Above is the author's rendition of hub doubling and machine doubling on coins.
The normal lettering and dates are shown above in the upper left. The machine doubling shown below and to the left reveals flat doubling. The drawing in the upper right shows notches and spaces with the doubling the same height as the normal letter and numbering.

The majority of encapsulated error coins are doubled die mintages with various degrees of doubling. The collector should be familiar with doubling by mint dies and machine doubling. Machine doubled coins do not command any additional value.

Above is a 1972-S machine double

Doubled die Coins in Circulation

A 1972 Doubled die Lincoln Cent

Above is a true doubled die cent. Note the doubling of the date is the same height in the numbers. All double dated coins have the same features as shown above.

Shown above is a 1959-D/D/D Lincoln cent

In the above photograph is a picture of a 1959 Lincoln cent with a triple D. Note the doubling all around the D.

1959-D Triple D (ANACS MS63, $154) (PCGS MS65, $26-$184) (PCGS MS66, $30-$116)

A PCGS 1960-D large date D over D

Among the doubling errors for the 1960 coins, there is a 1960 large date D over D. Others include DDO's for both large and small dates.

1960 D over D small over large date (PCGS MS65, $205) 2014

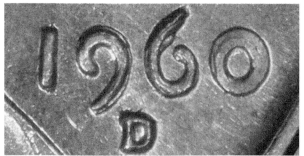

A PCGS 1960 Lincoln cent small date over large.

Form this photograph clearly the small zero is over the large zero. There are also noticeable doublings over the nine and the six.

1960 DDO Small over Large date (PCGS PR65, $299) (PCGS PR66, $276) (NGC PR67, $385), (PCGS PR68, $4600)

1960 DDO Large over Small Date (PCGS PR67, $300-$400), (PCGS PR68, $603-$1,006), (PCGS PR69, $7475)

1960-D DDO Small over Large Date (PCGS MS65 red, $658) 2014

1960-D DDO Large over Small Date (NGC PR64, $109) (NGC PR65, $138-$219) (NGC PR66, $161-253) (NGC PR67, $253-483)

1960-D DDO Small over Large Date (PCGS PR66, $276) 2014

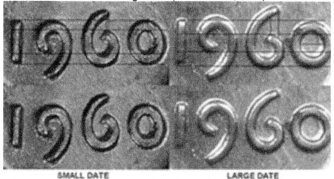

SMALL DATE   LARGE DATE

Above is a photograph of the comparison of the 1960 large and small dated coins.

A 1963-D DDO

Note in this coin the doubling of the D and a sharp doubling of the three.

1963-D DDO (PCGS MS64, $38) 2011

A 1964 doubled die reverse

Perhaps somewhat difficult to catch, there is doubling in the E.P.U and States.

1964 DDR (NGC MS62, $34)

Pictured above is a 1968-D over D Lincoln Cent

The D over D in the 1968 cent is clear enough to recognize without using a magnifying glass. As with most of the double mint marks, the coin sells for a reasonable amount in high mint state grades.

1968-D over D (PCGS MS65, $165) 2014

1968-D doubled die reverse

The best way to detect this coin error is to inspect the FC on the reverse of the coin. The doubling is very clear.

1968-D DDR (PCGS MS64, $100-250) 2016

1969-S Doubled die Lincoln cent

1969-S Lincoln cent doubled die

The two photographs above depict the famous and very valuable 1969-S doubled die Lincoln cent. Note the doubling of the lettering which is the same height throughout. The date doubling results with the numbers the same height.

1964 DDO Lincoln cent

Above is a 1964 Lincoln cent with strong doubling of AM and ES. The doubling of letters shows the raised lettering a feature of true doubling.

Some doubled die cents classify as "minor" and there are those considered as "major" errors. The minor errors will command less in the market verses those like the 1969-S doubled die Lincoln cent the command thousands.

Pictured above is a 1980 doubled die

One of the most difficult doubled dies to detect in the Lincoln cent coinage. There is doubling in the 80 and in the motto.

1980 DDO (PCGS MS64, $160-$600) (PCGS MS65, $1750) 2016

A 1982 doubled die Lincoln cent

The doubling occurs in the letters shown above and in the ONE.
1982 DDO large date die 2 (ANACS MS65, $21)

A 1983 doubled die obverse cent

There are many variations to the 1983 doubled die cent including DDR examples
1983 DDO (NGC MS64, $42-$70)

Above is a very distinct 1983 doubled die reverse
1983 DDR (PCGS MS64, $213) (NGC MS68, $3,220)

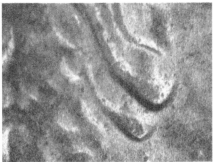
Double ear 1984 DDO

The 1984 Lincoln cent error is on Lincoln in the form of a double ear.

1984 DDO (ANACS MS62, $51) (PCGS MS65, $219) (PCGS MS66, $495) (PCGS MS67, $630-$805)

1995 Doubled die

The 1995 doubled die Lincoln cent is affordable for less than $50 depending on the grade. High grades of mint state command prices in excess of $50. The doubling on this coin is in LIBERTY with the doubling very pronounced in the B E and R. This coin would be difficult to locate in circulation.

1995 DDO (PCGS MS67, $69-$74) (PCGS MS68, $79)

1995-D Lincoln cent doubled die

The picture above represents a 1995-D DDO type 3 die reveals a heavily pronounced doubling of the WE, GO in GOD, and RU in the motto.

1995-D DDO (PCGS MS64, $300-$800) (PCGS MS65, $550-$1100)

A 1997 double ear Lincoln cent

First discovered many experts refused to agree that it was a true doubling. This coin error is now widely accepted as a die error.

1997 double ear (PCGS MS65, $195.50)

A 2006 Lincoln cent doubled die.

The 2006 doubled die Lincoln cent shows doubling most pronounced in the motto.

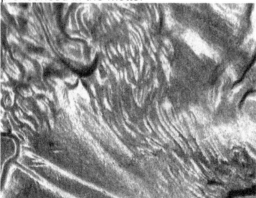

Above is a 2006 double ear Lincoln cent

Lincoln cents 1909-1958

There are numerous Lincoln cent errors dated 1909 through 1958. Since these coins are not common in circulation because the "wheat back" hoarding, it is difficult to locate errors from pocket change. Below are a number of Lincoln cent error coins that are of prominence in the collecting community.

The 1909-S issues have mintages with a double S. These coins noted as S over horizontal S. Coins range in value with grading as follows: (ANACS VG10, $89) (NGC MS63, $299-$345) (NGC MS64, $518) (PCGS MS65, $1006) (PCGS MS66, $2,070)

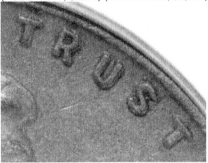

Above is an example of a 1917 doubled die.

The doubling is in the "We" and "TRUST" in the motto.

1917 DDO (PCGS G04 $69) (PCGS F12 $144) (raw EF40, $978) (PCGS MS66, $25,300-$28,750)

Above is a 1922 no D Lincoln cent.

Some of these coins circulated for a length of time since there are coins available in all grades. The reason that rare Lincoln cents before 1940 are available in the lowest grades is that coin collecting and the notable error coins were not recognized fully until the first coin guides circulated in the mid-nineteen-forties
1922 no D or partial D (PCGS G6, $250) (ANACS VG8, $800) (PCGS AU55, $4113) (PCGS MS63, $2500-$14,000)
(PCGS MS64, $40,000 - $70,000), (PCGS MS65, $100,000)

Above is a 1936 doubled die cent.

There are three variations of this doubled die coin with degrees of doubling. DDO type one contains doubling in the date, LIBERTY, and the motto and considered the strongest shown in the photographs above. DDO type two shows doubling in the date. DDO 3 shows doubling in the motto and the date but it is not very pronounced.

1936 proof type II DDO (PCGS MS66, $5,400-$5,750)
1936 DDO 2 (PCGS MS65, $3500) (PCGS MS66, $11,500-$21,850)
1936 DDO 3 (PCGS MS65, $1700)

Above is a 1943-D D over D 1943 D over D (PCGS MS65, $805- $2,530) (PCGS MS67, $4,500-$21,275)

Above is a PCGS sample of a 1943-S doubled die

From the photograph above the nine has apparent doubling. Some of the letters in LIBERTY show slight doubling.

1943-S DDO (PCGS MS67, 2325) 2015

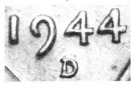

Photograph above is a 1944 D over S issue.
1944 D over S (PCGS MS66, $2,200- $16,100) (PCGS MS65, $5,100-$5,462.50)

The photograph above is a PCGS 1951-D over D Lincoln cent.

The best method of detecting this hub/die error is to review the five in the date clearly deformed with extra metal. The D over D is much less apparent but doubled slightly.

1951-D over D (ANACS AU58, $12) 2014
1951-D over S (PCGS, MS66, $230-$300), NGC MS67, $2350) 2014

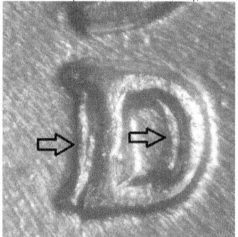
Above is a photograph of the D over D in the 1953-D Lincoln cent.
1953 D over D (PCGS MS65, $79) 2014

1953 proof doubled die with distinct doubling in LIBERTY

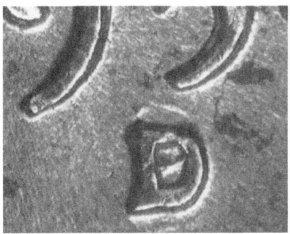

Above is a PCGS 1954 D/D/D mint error

The photograph above reveals a DDD triple error for the 1954 Lincoln cent. For the novice the appearance of this error does not provide a clear depiction of a triple D.

1954 D/D/D (ANACS MS65, $130) 2014

1955 Doubled die

One of the most sought after doubled die cents is the 1955. This coin was one of the first Lincoln cents to stir up collectors into seeking this coin. Most of these coins are in AU or mint state condition and this error coin quickly left circulation. The values of this coin range from $2000 to $10,000 for various grades in mint state condition. This coin is the most extreme of all doubled die mintages. Coin collecting in the 1950's was skyrocketing with the public and a passion for collecting was born.

1955 Doubled die Lincoln cent

A 1955-D doubled die cent

The 1955-D doubled die shows a doubling of the one and the nine in the date. This coin does not command a large premium but it is a collectable error.
1955-D DDO (ANACS MS64, $42)

Pictured above is a 1955 S/S/S

This is a perfect triple S coin. Note how distinct the three S's are.
1955-S Triple S RPM (PCGS MS64, $32-$92) RPM (ANACS MS65, $127) RPM (NGC MS66, $60)

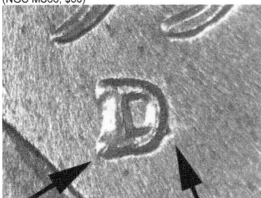

Pictured above is a PCGS 1956 DDS cent

This photograph reveals that there is a missed stamping but it is not entirely clear to see the D, D, S striking. Since the coin is a PCGS example, no questions for the experts.

1956 D/D/S (ANACS MS64, $40) 2014

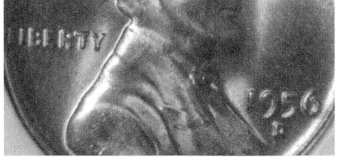

Above is a 1956-D D over D Lincoln cent. Value $50-100

A 1958 doubled die Lincoln cent
The coin has very strong doubling in the motto and LIBERTY.

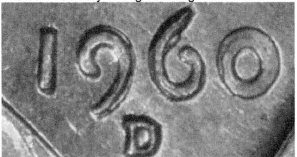

Above is a 1960 D over D – approximate value is $800

Above is a D over horizontal D.

1963-D Doubled die obverse. Strongest in the Motto – Value $25

1966 DDO – primarily in LIBERTY. Considered as a minor DDO

Above is a 1969-S doubled die cent. This coin can sell in excess of $50,000 in AU or better condition.

Above is a 1971 DDO – doubled LIBERTY

1971-S DDO. Value in mint state ranges from $250-$500.

Above is an example of a 1972 doubled die – Value can exceed $7,000

Very rare 1974 Aluminum Lincoln cent. Only one known to exist.

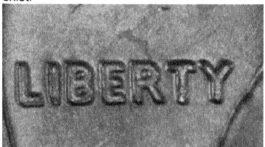

1980 DDO. Strong doubling in LIBERTY –value exceeds $1500 in MS65 or better.

Above is a 1983 doubled die reverse, which can sell for over $1700.

1984 DDO Doubled ear and double beard

Above is a 1992-D close AM. The close AM contains letters that are touching each other as opposed to a clear separation.

Photographs above show doubling for the 1995-D Lincoln cent.

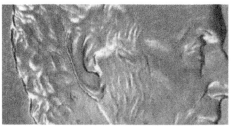

1997 double ear – This error can sell for $150 or more in MS65.

2006 DDO doubling in LIBERTY PCGS MS65 $50

2014 DDO doubling in LIBERTY. Value $150 MS64

BIE errors

Above is a "BIE" cent

A common error occurred with the Lincoln cents, especially in the 1950's. There is a distinct amount of extra material between the B and the E thus the notation of "BIE". There are full BIE coins such as the one shown above and partial BIE coins. The value of a BIE coin is generally less than $5. A large amount of BIE coins can be located in the 1950's, especially 1951-D, 1954-S, 1955-D, 1955-S, 1956, 1957, and 1957-D. Later dated BIE common coins include 1960-D, 1994 and 1995

Above is a full 1955 BIE error

BIE errors are common and come in various types of fills between the B and the E in Liberty. The best BIE error is a full line as shown in the first photograph above. There are many types of BIE errors for each date of occurrence.
BIE errors need to be uncirculated to obtain any significant value.

Wide AM Lincoln Cents

Located in proof sets, the discovery of some 1990 Lincoln cents without the S. About 300 of these coins exist with values exceeding $4000.

Until 1992, the US Mint manufactured cents with the wide AM. All 1993 and after issues intended to have a close AM for circulation. All proof Lincoln Cents issued from 1993 to 2009 should have the AM of America separated from one another. However, some proof 1998 and 1999 examples with the letters AM of America close to each other or almost touching exist, which indicates a mint state die used in place of a proof die. Since 1993, there have been several dates with both the wide and close AM. A 1992 with a close AM is extremely rare. In proof sets, both the wide and close AM occur in 1998 and 1999. There are circulating examples of wide AM coins dated 1998 and 1999 along with the 2000 wide and close AM which is most common.

2000 wide AM

The most common of all wide verses close AM's is the 2000-S proof set coin. The wide AM sells under $10

1999-S Wide AM – close AM

The 1999 Lincoln cents minted with two variations. The wide AM and the close AM, differentiated by the AM touching letters and a space between the A and the M.

The close AM can command $60 or more in various proof state conditions. The close AM is common in circulation intended coins.

1998-S wide AM – close AM

The 1998-S wide and close AM appears in proof sets. The 1998 close AM mint state encapsulated coin can sell in excess of $500

1992 close AM Only about 10 known examples. Very rare

1992-D close AM

Extremely rare to date. One of these coins sold at Heritage Auctions in AU condition for $5,640. The first coin located sold at HA for over $20,000 in MS64 condition.

For collectors searching for these errors, it will not be an easy task since the valuable errors reside in proof sets except for the very rare 1992-D.

There are numerous examples of Lincoln cents escaping the copper plating process in the US Mint resulting in partial of fully zinc coins in circulation. A wide range of prices exists for these coins, some in excess of $100 and others sell for less than $30. The weight of a normal Lincoln-copper plated zinc cent is 2.5 grams. Any coin missing the plating should weigh slightly under 2.5 grams.

There is the ability to take a copper-coated cent and plate it to give it the appearance that it is missing the copper coating. Coins that are plated will gain some weight and will therefore exceed 2.5 grams. Be careful of fakes.

Lincoln cents missing clad layer

Authenticated 1999-D missing copper layer

There have been examples found of 1983 Lincoln cents that have been minted on copper planchets. These coins weigh around 3.11 grams, which is the intended weight of all copper cents dated before 1982 and some 1982 issues.

Above is an authentic photograph of a 1983 copper cent.
At auction, this coin will sell in excess of $16,000.

Jefferson Nickel DDR and DDO

Doubled die Jefferson nickels errors are not as frequent as Lincoln cents and the number of error dates are lower.

Above is an example of a 1938 D over D Jefferson nickel. Value is approximately $100 in MS65 condition.

Above is an example of a 1939 double MONTICELLO. The MS67 example sold over in excess of $2300

1943 3 over 2 Jefferson nickel
Prices for this coin in mint state can exceed $2500

Above is the 1949-D over S Jefferson nickel. This coin can command thousands in mint sate conditions. Mint state $8000

Above is a 1953 DDO . The doubling on this coin is not extremely pronounced. The motto is most apparent. $90 mint state.

Roosevelt Dime DDR and DDO

Below are a few doubled die Roosevelt dimes to give the collector an idea of how to spot doubled dies in this series.

Mercury dime 1940-S doubled die date. Value $50-250 depending on the condition of the coin.

Mercury dime 2 over 1 – Wide range of values depending on the condition of the coin.

Above is a 1964-D over D Roosevelt dime . Value $50.

1968-S Double S mint state $50

1968-S Doubled die reverse mint state $25

1968 Roosevelt dime no S
Some mint sets contained 1968 Roosevelt dimes with no S. Only 12 known to exist with a value of $12,000 or more.

1975-no S
The 1975 no S Roosevelt dime can be located in proof sets.
Only two known to exist selling in excess of $375,000

The mint used the 1968 proof reverse die to mint coins for circulation in 1968, 1969, and 1970. Below are the photographs of the two die reverses. The most noticeable difference is in the lines in the torch with deeply grooved lines in the flame.

Normal reverse of a Roosevelt dime for circulation

Proof reverse of 1968

182

Washington quarter errors

Above is a 1946-s over S Washington quarter. The S over S is slightly apparent. Value $50-$100

1965 DDO Washington quarter – mint state $575
The 1965 doubled die Washington quarter show doubling in "IN GOD WE TRUST" and other lettering around the coin.

1967 SMS[28] DDO Washington quarter – minor doubling in LIBERTY-$150 in mint state.

Above is a 1969-D over D doubled die. Value depending on grade $25-$50.

1776-1976 Washington quarter DDO - minor doubling in LIBERTY. PCGS AU58 $690

---

[28] SMS - Special mint set

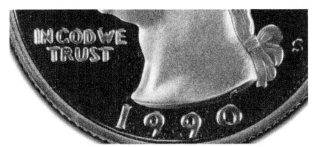

1990-S with strong doubling in the words IN GOD WE TRUST.

2004-D Extra Leaf high shown just below the larger leaf on the left.

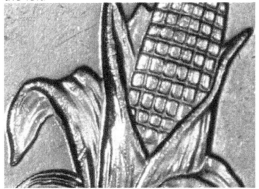

2004-D Extra left low shown just below the larger leaf on the left.
Both coins above can yield $150 or more in mint state conditions.

Half Dollar Doubled dies and Oddities

Above is the 1946 doubled die half dollar mint state value $7000

Above is a 1955 Bugs Bunny Half

The lips of Franklin contain several lines.
Value approximately $200 in mint sate

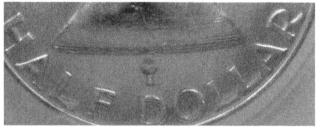

Above is a 1959 DDR Franklin half. The doubling is primarily in the D and the O in DOLLAR. Value $80

Above is a 1964 Kennedy half with accented hair. Value-$50-$100.

Above is a 1964-D over D Kennedy half – Value $100.

1965 DDR with doubling primarily in the word UNITED.

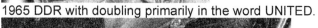

Above is a 1966 Kennedy Half Doubled die -mint state $25

188

1967 DDR doubling pronounced in UNITED – Value mint state $25

1971 DDO Kennedy half doubling in WE TRUST Value $100 in mint state conditions

1973-D Kennedy Half DDO. Minor doubling in LIBERTY- Value MS65-$200

1974-D DDO Kennedy half. Primarily in WE TRUST. Value $45-150 mint state conditions.

1776-1976 proof half DDR (PCGS MS65, $500)

1977-D Kennedy half minor doubling in IN GOD WE TRUST.
PCGS MS65 $650

Dollar errors

A truly rare and unique dollar with no S. Only one coin known to exist.

Amazing 2000 W dollar coin minted with 22 K gold. Only 39 of these minted. Twenty-seven melted by the mint and the remaining 12 were sent into space on the space shuttle Columbia and upon return were sent to Fort Knox.

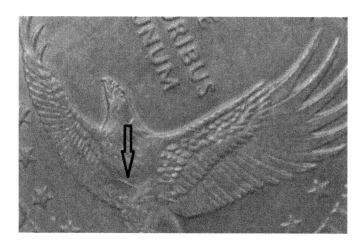

There are examples of a die break that appears as an arrow through the eagle on the reverse of the 2000-P Sacagawea dollar.

The 2000 Dollar placed into boxes of Cheerios. Mintage occurred on 22 KT gold in error. Coin values range from $4000 - $6000.

References:
- The Official American Numismatic Association Grading Standards for United States Coins" edited by Kenneth Bressett.
- The US Mint site – www.usmint.org
- The Lincoln cent resource – www.lincolncentresource.com

Glossary

ANA – American Numismatic Association. The ANA provides insights to coin collecting. Anyone can join ANA for a small fee.

Blank – A raw planchet that is ready for striking.

Clipped Planchet – A raw blank missing part of the circumference or other portion of the coin is a clipped planchet.

Brockage - A brockage is a Mint error, an early capped die impression where a sharp incused image has been left on the next coin fed into the coining chamber. Most brockages are partial; full brockages are rare and the most desirable form of the error.[29]

Cud – A die break usually found around the circumference of the coin.

Denomination – The face value of a coin or bill. The Lincoln cent denomination is one cent.

Die – A die is a punch that contains a face of the design used to imprint on a planchet.

Die crack – A raised line appears on the surface of a coin as the metal fills in where the die has cracked.

Die Errors - Die errors caused by the mint dies wearing down over time or dies that have not been prepared identical to others.

DDO – The designation for coins that contain a doubled die obverse

DDR – The designation for coins that contain a doubled die reverse.

DMM – double mint- mark

Doubled die – A distinct doubling of the lettering and or the date on a coin created from the dies.

eBay – An auction site designed for people to buy and sell various items.

Flow lines – There are lines shown of the surface of the coin caused by the spreading of the metal in striking.

Heritage Auctions – A company that sells items on line and through live auctions.

---

[29] PCGS Term from PCGS.com

Hub – The punch used to create the dies used to press the design on a coin. The design is opposite of the actual die image.
Mint Mark – The mint places a letter on most coins to represent the site of mintage.
D – Denver
S – San Francisco
P – Philadelphia (also no min- mark)
W – West Point
CC – Carson City
O – New Orleans
Mint Striking Errors - Collectors and organizations dedicated to collecting coins' regard mint striking errors as those created by the minting process. Most of these coins command no significant value, especially those that have no date. DDO – A coin with doubling on the obverse relates doubled die obverse.
DDR – A coin with doubling on the reverse - a doubled die reverse.
MPD –A date or multiple dates appear in different places on the coin.
Mule – A coin that minted on the incorrect planchet is a mule.
Numismatist – A person that studies and accumulates knowledge of coins is a numismatist.
Obverse – The front of a coin
Off center – A coin that struck outside of the collar that holds the coin in place for minting.
OMM – Over mint- mark – coins that are stuck with one mint mark and then a different mint mark.
Over dates – One date on the coin is over or under another date.
Planchet – The blank annealed that to make a coin
Planchet Error – A coin minted with a defective blank considered a planchet error.
RPM – Re-punched mint mark. The mint takes dies that are of one mint- mark and re-punches the die with another mint-mark. Traces of the original mint- mark remain creating an error coin.
Sandwich Coin – The interior of a coin is one alloy covered by another alloy on both sides. Modern day silver coins contain copper interiors with silver plating on both sides.

Variations - Variations are not mint errors in the technical sense. Variations in coins caused by creating hubs and dies that are not exactly the same resulting in dates that can be compared as large to small, wide to thin etc.
Whizzing – The process of using high-pressure water and brushes to clean the surface of a coin noted as whizzing. Whizzing significantly reduces the value of a coin.

Saddle Strike – A coin struck with opposite sides protruding from the coin giving the appearance of a saddle

We want to answer all questions pertaining to coins or the content of this guide. Please feel free to email us at: McDonald.Stan@comcast.net

CPSIA information can be obtained
at www.ICGtesting.com
Printed in the USA
BVOW06s1035170917
495106BV00014B/136/P